THE COMPLETE GUIDE TO

SUCCESSFUL EVENT PLANNING

Shannon Kilkenny

THE COMPLETE GUIDE TO
SUCCESSFUL EVENT PLANNING

Copyright © 2006 by Atlantic Publishing Group, Inc.
1210 SW 23rd Place • Ocala, Florida 34474 • 800-814-1132 • 352-622-5836–Fax
Web site: www.atlantic-pub.com • E-mail: sales@atlantic-pub.com
SAN Number: 268-1250

ISBN-13: 978-0-910627-92-4   ISBN-10: 0-910627-92-4

Library of Congress Cataloging-in-Publication Data

Kilkenny, Shannon, 1955-
  The complete guide to successful event planning / by Shannon Kilkenny.
      p. cm.
  Includes bibliographical references and index.
  ISBN-13: 978-0-910627-92-4 (alk. paper)
  ISBN-10: 0-910627-92-4 (alk. paper)
  1. Special events--Planning--Handbooks, manuals, etc. 2. Special events--Management--Handbooks, manuals, etc. 3. Meetings--Planning--Handbooks, manuals, etc. 4. Congresses and conventions--Planning--Handbooks, manuals, etc. 5. Special events industry--Vocational guidance--Handbooks, manuals, etc. I. Title.

  GT3405.K55 2006
  394.2--dc22
                          2006035557

COVER DESIGN: Meg Buchner • megadesn@mchsi.com
INTERIOR LAYOUT DESIGN & PRODUCTION: Studio 6 Sense • info@6sense.net
EDITOR/ PROOFREADER: Marie Lujanac • mlujanac817@yahoo.com

Printed in the United States

Contents

Section 3: Greening Your Event

Section 4: High Level Logistics

Section 7: Appendix

"A successful event or seminar takes a clear vision and an enormous amount of planning, details and follow up. Successful Event Planning is a valuable resource and a "must have" for any department or organization that puts on events or seminars – regardless of size."

Karen R. McLaughlin, APR, CEO
QB Comm, Inc., Rochester, NY

"The organization and systems outlined and recommended in this Guide have enabled us to produce greater and more successful events, enhanced the experience for our clients and increased profitability for our business. Kudos to Shannon!"

Katrinka McKay, Innkeeper and General Manager,
Sebastopol, CA

"Wow! This is what I do for a living!!! It's really gratifying to see things I do daily put into words and even better to know there's a great resource to use when I get stuck".

Siobhan Coen, CMP
Autodesk, San Rafael, CA

"As an event producer for dozens of years, I've found Shannon's complete guide most informative and compelling…. And I thought I knew it all!!!"

Meta Mehling
Meta Mehling & Associates, Cupertino, CA

"Whether you are on your 1st or 500th event, Successful Event Planning is a book that I suggest you have. The plan for success is in your hand, all you have to do is follow it. I have incorporated this information into my project planning for every event. Obviously a true professional wrote this because it's so complete."

Katherine Lucas, Real Estate Entrepreneur
Columbus, OH and Naples, FL

Author Dedication

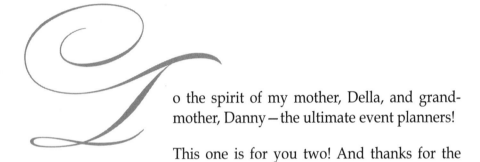

To the spirit of my mother, Della, and grand-mother, Danny — the ultimate event planners!

This one is for you two! And thanks for the happy gene.

Acknowledgements

 his book, many years in the making, is the culmination of my life story. And what an adventurous event it has been! To those who weaved into and out of my story — I acknowledge you and thank you for enlightening my world. Extraordinary thanks to those who settled in and participated in shaping the person I am today. I appreciate every encouraging and inspiring word and even the not so encouraging but truthful and honest evaluations — all were valuable.

A few friends stepped up to assist me when I was waning with this book. Thank you, Cindy Morgan, for proofing my material and keeping me focused when it was important — timing is everything. To Jane Grossenbacher who helped me with words when mine were failing me — I am thankful.

My deepest appreciation goes to Kate Currey for her total and ongoing support and spirit in just about everything. She helped me in more ways than she will ever know.

A few others need to be mentioned for their friendship, inspiration, and support: My brother Mark, Guy Morgan, Sharon Call, Suzanne Hart (in memory of), all of my Kampers, Lovey Glady, and of course the members of my Book Club. Your consistent and unrelenting support has been lovingly noted.

To my esteemed peers and colleagues—thank you. You keep me motivated and challenged to continue rising to any occasion and remind me of what excellence looks like. And to the storytellers in this book, I honor your time and value your contribution.

And to you dear clients, thank you for your trust, faith, confidence, flexibility, and appreciation. You encourage me to keep coming back!

And I can't forget Cayanne who shows me love everyday, albeit conditional, as any good cat will do. She keeps me responsible.

We all have choices, make good ones! Make everyday a joyful event!

taging an event is an art. In essence you don't plan a party – you design it. Planning an event is like producing a play. The venue is the stage. The event planner is the director. Whether working with a professional or on your own, *The Complete Guide to Successful Event Planning* will help you articulate a mood, focus your vision, and achieve your objective.

Events mark some of life's most sentimental and important moments. Ensuring their success requires confidence, strategy, organization – AND – this book.

When did you last plan an event? You are likely to say that it has been a very long time – or perhaps never! But think again. An event is not just a wedding or a public victory campaign celebration. It may be your partner's 60th birthday celebration. It may be a board meeting for 20 or a spiritual gathering for several hundred.

Even if you are a seasoned planner and are comfortable organizing events of all types, this book has comprehensive information and tricks of the trade that you may have yet to discover.

How often have we had an inspiring idea for that perfect event or been asked in our professional lives to produce a complicated corporate event with little lead time? Did we panic in frustration or confusion about what to do first or what to do next? Shannon provides a step-by-step guide so that your event will be a success, no matter what the obstacle.

The decision to plan an event becomes the canvas onto which you apply your ideas and vision. Shannon has provided a palette of colors to choose from.

The most difficult part of any event is transforming the idea or inspiration into your own personal signature. The execution is all about attention to detail. She guides you from uncertainty and confusion into confidence about your own sense of style, and she encourages you to take calculated risks for the perfect and memorable event.

Throughout my 25-year career in public relations, I have been fortunate to be called upon by Fortune 500 CEOs, heads of state, presidents and governors, academic institutions and even the United Nations to design and execute events in all kinds and sizes throughout the world.

No two events are ever the same, and in no way can you prevent unforeseen obstacles from finding you. Trust me – they will.

Shannon Kilkenny has provided us with all the necessary tools for successful event planning. Just as important, she demonstrates how to enjoy the process. She lives her life with the same passion, determination, and pride that you will find within these pages. She lets nothing stop her on her journey to success and happiness.

So sit back and read on. Trust your creative instincts and let this book guide you through your current and future events.

Cindy Testa-McCullagh
President, McCullagh and Company

Cindy serves as the Director of Public Affairs for the Shorenstein Company, a privately held owner and operator of commercial real estate nationwide. She is responsible for tenant, employee, and community relations on a local and national level and the development and implementation of programs in support of the Shorenstein family's extensive political, civic, academic and philanthropic interests.

She has been involved in strategic planning and production of such events as the 1988 – 2004 Democratic National Conventions; the 1992 and 1996 Presidential Inaugurations; served on the Democratic National Committee Site Selection Board for the 2000 National Convention; the United Nations 50th Anniversary Commemorative Ceremonies in 1995 in San Francisco; the 2002 World Economic Forum – Davos; the 2003 Inaugural Committee for Governor Ed Rendell in Pennsylvania and the 2004 SF Mayoral Transition/Swearing in Committee for San Francisco Mayor Gavin Newsom; was a delegate to APEC (Asia Pacific Economic Cooperation) in Kuala Lumpur, New Zealand and Mexico; she worked closely on the planning and implementing of the New Economy Forum with the Haas School of Business at UC Berkeley/Dean Laura Tyson and the Shorenstein Forum at the Asia Pacific Research Center at Stanford University; serves as a co-chair of the Prohibition Documentary Advisory Committee, a project developed in conjunction with the Wine Institute and sponsored by the Bancroft Library at University of California at Berkeley. Cindy also is a member of the Council of the Friends of the Bancroft Library at UC Berkeley.

Cindy participated in the planning and executing the Clinton Global Initiative in New York 2005 and 2006. Together with Harvard University, Cindy organized a group of graduate students from the Business, Design, Government and Law schools designing a redevelopment program of the Broadmoor neighborhood devastated by Hurricane Katrina.

Cindy was also involved in the development of Harvard University Kennedy School of Government Corporate Social Responsibility Program and Conference Series held in San Francisco, New York, and Washington DC in conjunction with The Conference Board of NY, ChevronTexaco, General Motors, Pfizer, Abbott, InBev, and The Coca-Cola Company.

About This Book

Introduction

Whenever two or more people are gathered, it is an event. Events and event planning have been happening since the beginning of civilization. One could say that event planning, bringing people together for a specific reason, is the oldest profession.

In every organization, there are events in the process of being organized every day. It is a never-ending cycle. The number of events and different types of events happening is staggering. Millions of people around the world are participating in organized events right now as you read this.

Maybe you have worked on an event in one capacity or another, either as a volunteer or as a paid employee. Perhaps you participated in planning your high school reunion or a fundraiser for your children's art department. Maybe you did some campaigning for a local politician or you planned a seminar to promote your own business. When it was over, did you think of steps that could have gone smoother?

Who is in charge of all these thousands of events every day? Planners. Some events are wildly successful and some fall short. This book is designed to assist both the novice and the well-seasoned event planners to become better organizers and save time, money, and hours of frustration. By using this book to learn from others' experiences, you can enjoy your next event. Event planning is a truly fun and exciting endeavor. This book is intended to make your life easier by giving you step-by-step guidance.

There is no such thing as a perfect or flawless event. Every event will have something go wrong. Remember Murphy's Law, "If something can go wrong, it will." Something will be missing, things will change at the last minute, or something unexpected will happen, but a good planner will find the solution and create an illusion so that the people attending the event will never know. This guide will prepare you for some of those possibilities. They can be as small as forgetting birthday candles for the cake or a catastrophic incident such as a hurricane hitting your meeting site for 30,000 participants.

MY STORY

When I started in the event planning business many years ago, there were no books or classes on the subject and very few mentors to call upon for advice. It was not even a profession with job titles at the time. There were no professional organizations with tests and certifications or magazines dedicated to the trade. Most events were just assigned to the most reliable person who may or may not have had the time or experience. Fortunately I love to gather people. I was a natural, but I had to make my own mistakes and learn literally standing or running on my own two feet. I loved it. And you have to love it, or do not do it!

I have been coordinating events for more than 26 years, and I still love it. I have directed, produced, and coordinated events in every category of the event industry. There were numerous events in the corporate market, industry shows, spectacular special events, and hundreds of social events. Each event was entirely different and prepared me for the next. I learned along the way, mostly through trial and error. Through each job, I learned something new about a different aspect of the trade. It was my path of development that got me here today as an author.

This Guide is For You

Welcome to the fabulous world of event planning! If you have an event, meeting, or party to produce, plan, or coordinate, you have come to the right place. Events do not just happen by themselves; they are well planned, specifically orchestrated, and extremely coordinated. This is what you will learn from this guide. Preparation is the key to any successful event. Remember, we as planners are responsible for the education, entertainment, feeding, housing, safety, and care of all attending or participating in our events.

This practical guide is designed and dedicated to saving you time, money, and frustration, without omitting any of the necessary steps. It will provide the particulars that make up the big picture of event planning, giving you advice, opinions, suggestions, tried and true methods, hints, tips, instructions, and organizational plans. It will take you from the concept to the thank-you notes. We've included real life stories to motivate you to get started on your own event.

There is always something new or different to enhance the logistics and creativity of planning an event. Things are changing all the time, whether it is new technology, new ways to "green" your event, Web or Internet services and applications, new or remodeled venues, contracts, or insurance laws; it is wise to keep up with new developments in all of these areas. Even if you have been directing events for a long time, this book may teach you a new thing or two. Constant and continuing education is a common sense necessity in today's ever changing landscape.

For those of you new to event planning, this book will direct your moves, help organize your time, provide you with resources and suggestions, keep you focused, and allow you to look as though you have been an event planner for years. Best of all, it may keep you from making the costly and time-consuming mistakes thousands of planners have made before you. Just one or two of the tips suggested in this book can save you a large percent of money on one event alone and possibly save your job as well! Just read, follow, listen, learn, and be flexible. One of the most important characteristics of an event planner is flexibility. It is part of the job. We want to make the planning experience a fun and thrilling time for you because there is always room for one more successful event planner in this vast and infinite world of events.

SCOPE

The information in this guide is applicable to all events whether it is the Academy Awards, Uncle Steve's 60th birthday party, or the annual conference for the Sierra Club. Each event has distinct characteristics, but they all have common threads weaving in and out of the planning process. These universal threads are only one aspect of what this guide presents. We introduce and lead you through step by step details essential to designing and producing successful, memorable and extraordinary events. We help you make smart decisions during the entire process so that you are not reinventing the wheel.

We cannot cover everything you need to know about event planning or prepare you for all surprises, but we do offer the groundwork, a solid base of helpful information. It is your job to build on this foundation. Basic materials, tools, and the draft schematics are provided; you bring in the subcontractors, work with the players, create the timelines, create and maintain the budget, and execute the details.

How and When to Use this Guide

There are several ways to get the most out of this guide. You can use it at any stage of your planning process from the concept to the day of the event! Read it from cover to cover or go directly to a section relevant to your current circumstance or to complete a particular task. Wherever you are in the process, from the creation stage or deep into the details, you can find help in this book. Use it wisely and often. Keep it handy for reference, ideas, and suggestions. You will be glad you did.

Although the sections are in sequence in this book, they may not necessarily follow the flow or pertain to the decisions and strategies for your specific event. Event planning is not a linear process. One action does not necessarily or logically come after another. Some decisions are made simultaneously, while some must be subsequent to others. The process is different with each individual event. As you go through this guide and begin coordinating your event, you will understand. For instance, you cannot create the marketing material and begin your promotional efforts before you know where the event will be held. You need to know the dates and times and before you select a site. You cannot invite the keynote speaker or book the entertainment until the goals and objectives and defined vision for the event have been established. Even though events may not follow a defined sequence, the planning process can be simplified and organized if the guidelines and suggestions in this book are followed and close attention is paid to each step along the way.

There is some repetition of the content in the sections and chapters that is unavoidable. Planning involves activities that are not isolated but are interrelated. Consequently each chapter, while integral to the whole, is also an independent component.

Benefits to the Reader

Some specifics this book will do for you:

- Save you time and money.

- Develop your organizational skills.

- Eliminate the guesswork.

- Enhance your wealth of knowledge about the event planning business.

- Answer common questions with tried and true solutions.

- Offer ideas and suggestions.

- Help you work within the constraints of time, materials, and money.

- Provide dozens of resources.

- Help define roles and responsibilities.

- Provide options to accomplish many tasks.

- Help you make intelligent decisions.

- Assist you in becoming a master in money-saving techniques.

- Teach you to enjoy the process because you are prepared.

- Make you efficient and competent.

- Provide skillful negotiating techniques.

- Prepare you to wear many hats and juggle simultaneous tasks.

- Make your efforts timely and systematic.

- Relieve frustration.

- Prepare you for the unexpected.

INTENDED AUDIENCE

Anyone who is planning an event will benefit from this guide! It is chock full of solutions and experience whether you are an administrative assistant, CEO, executive secretary, professional business person, manager, business owner, travel coordinator, an independent meeting planner, or just starting out in the meeting planning industry.

Whether you work in a business, organization, association, non-profit, the hospitality industry, or whatever you do, wherever you work, reading this book will be worth your time. You have valuable experience, great skills, and natural talent required to become a great planner! We intend to enhance what you know and channel those talents into creating gratifying and rewarding events.

Too often the task of coordinating an event is given to the inexperienced, over-worked employee. Maybe you have been assigned, hired, asked to coordinate, or have made the choice to put on an event. It may be job-related, a volunteer commitment with an association, an organization, a church or social event; it might be your daughter's wedding or your partner's surprise 50th birthday party. It could be a four-day conference for 2,500 or an afternoon workshop for 20. It does not matter why you are doing it or what you are doing, or whom you are doing it for, you will soon become the definitive multi-tasking planner.

WHAT SHOULD WE CALL IT?

Since "events" is a general word for hundreds of types of gatherings, it is difficult to focus or home in on one or two specific types. We will speak about all events because they have a common element: a gathering of people for a specific purpose.

Throughout this book when planning techniques differ between business/educational events or social/special events, we will describe the differences and make suggestions for each type. For example, finding the appropriate venue for a three-day conference will differ greatly from searching for the right venue for a concert or perhaps a wedding that takes place in a single day or perhaps lasts for only a few hours. All three types of events need equal organization, care, and precise planning, but the planning process may vary enough for a mention in this book.

The following chapter will help put into perspective the differences between business meetings/educational events and social/special events.

The job titles — coordinator, planner, producer, manager, director — are all used interchangeably. They all mean the person in charge of the day — to-day, hands-on business of planning an event, the one who makes it happen! The same goes for the actions such as coordinating, planning, and producing: they mean the act of doing your job. For the people participating in your event, we use a variety of words such as guest, participant, attendee, member, ticket holder, employee, or audience.

USING CHECKLISTS AND TIMELINES

Sample checklists and timelines located in the *Appendix* and on **the companion CD-ROM** serve as important planning tools in nearly every step in the process. They are extremely helpful in keeping you focused and on track. They are samples only, and you are encouraged to edit them to your specific needs since not all tasks will be appropriate for your specific event.

Checklists guarantee that significant and essential tasks and details are dealt with in a timely manner. Think of the checklist as an opportunity to double check everything, leaving all questions answered and tasks done. When the tasks and details on the sample checklists are not appropriate to your event, tailor them to fit your own needs and goals.

Timelines will become your best friend if you use them. They are reminders for what needs to be done and when to do it. They are another essential tool to ensure everything is covered. The complexity or simplicity of your timeline will be determined by the size and length of your event and, of course, your personality type.

Use these timelines and checklists for yourself, with your staff, committees, vendors and suppliers, and anyone else involved in the process. They are useful in your meetings, delegating responsibilities, working with vendors, and designing and publishing marketing material. They are also useful when writing the summary report at the end of the event. Good lists with notations and dates are very useful in summing up every aspect of the event when it is over.

STORIES AND PERSONAL EXPERIENCES

Many of the stories come from my own and my colleagues' experiences. They show how quick action can save an event. Often when something unplanned arises and the planner scrambles for the "fix," participants are unaware of any near-disaster. That is the sign of a great planner. These stories are true. You can learn from our mishaps, our on-the-run solutions, and perhaps get a chuckle or two.

MONEY SAVING TIPS

Where appropriate, chapters will include money-saving tips, sometimes within a specific topic. Some are negotiable with your vendors such as venues or hotels, your caterers, or with the transportation industry. Some are ideas for using local talent or services. They are only suggestions but know that they have worked. For instance, do not be afraid to ask for discounts, freebies, or extras. All experienced planners do. You will be amazed at what you can get with a smile and a courteous request.

ENVIRONMENTAL SUGGESTIONS

Throughout each chapter we offer suggestions, tips, and resources to transform your event into a more progressive and environmentally resourceful product. We have suggestions that you may build upon to create your own environmental standards to use when working with others in the industry. There is an extensive chapter dedicated to environmental planning that you can take pride in when you see the enormous impact that results when "greening" the way you do business.

GLOBAL CONSIDERATIONS

Our world is shrinking so that we must pay attention to the globalization of the event planning industry and keep up with the latest trends, cultural diversity, laws, and regulations in events world wide. When appropriate, information will be integrated into the chapter or will appear at the end of the chapter to provide an international perspective on event planning.

THE APPENDIX

The Appendix in this book contains timelines and checklists for all occasions, hundreds of Internet resources, and a glossary of common words used in the event planning industry.

BOOK DISCLAIMER

Event planning covers an enormous amount of information, and every event is unique. We offer you the fundamentals and suggest that you continue to learn by checking the resources listed in the back of this book.

May your events be successful, may your goals and objectives be met, and may your events be win-win situation for all. Remember, enjoy yourself, keep smiling, and have fun!

The Anatomy
of An Event

Even today's awesome technology is not a substitute for the magic that occurs with teamwork, sharing, and networking when people get together in one space. Coming together for a common purpose changes how people feel. It creates an environment that envelops participants and influences them consciously and subconsciously.

The word event means an occasion, a gathering of people at a certain place at a certain time for a specific reason. Each occasion can be called something different, but we will use the word "event" regularly and other synonyms as appropriate. The names change, but the planning process remains the same.

Differences between events are typically: why your participants come together, who your attendees are, the type of event you organize, its location, and the goals you want to meet. We are gathering people for a common event that is planned, organized, and detailed. You can successfully use the techniques in this book regardless of what you call it, where you hold it, or how many participants you have. The importance lies in the similarities of events, using your skills, talent, and experience to produce and manage these events successfully.

Events often combine social, business, and educational aspects, but most fall into one of the following groups.

SPECIAL AND SOCIAL EVENTS

The largest and broadest category of events, special events can be open to the public at large with no admission requirements or specify a target audience with a registration fee. The size, shape, and purpose of a special or social event are as assorted as the venues they are held in. They can range from the Presidential Inauguration in the nation's capital, to a clam bake at the local yacht club; from the LPG Tournament to the high school fundraiser for new band uniforms; from a Farm Aid concert to Guy's science fair. The examples that follow are a partial list of special and social events:

SOCIAL OR SPECIAL EVENTS		
• Anniversaries	• Expositions	• Political rallies
• Art Exhibits	• Fairs	• Reunions
• Auctions	• Fashion shows	• Road shows
• Award banquets	• Festivals	• School functions
• Book signings	• Fundraisers	• Showers
• Ceremonies	• Historic reenactments	• Sporting events
• Cocktail receptions	• Galas	• Trade shows
• Community programs	• Golf Tournaments	• Tributes
• Concerts	• Parades	• Weddings

BUSINESS AND EDUCATIONAL EVENTS

These events are typically corporate, industry, or educational related and are geared toward like-minded, work-oriented people. Usually they are specifically designed for a type of industry, certain topics, particular businesses, or training. They are rarely open to the public but are reserved for peers, clients, students, customers, trades people, and associated industry or businesses and often have an educational element. They may include vendors, suppliers, services, and sales departments. These types of events are usually organized within the corporation, association, or organization. Business and educational events include but are not limited to:

BUSINESS OR EDUCATIONAL EVENTS		
• Board meetings	• Intensives	• Sessions
• Classes	• Lectures	• Shareholder meetings
• Clinics	• Meetings	• Symposiums
• Conferences	• Retreats	• Trainings
• Conventions	• Sales meetings	• Workshops
• Forums	• Seminars	

WHY PEOPLE MEET

The reasons people gather for events are as diverse as the people who attend them. Ensure that your goals and objectives for your event include one or more of the following reasons. You want to inspire, motivate, and entice people to come and participate. A few motivating factors to gather people are:

WHY PEOPLE MEET		
• Annual meetings	• Force of habit	• Milestones
• Appreciation dinners	• Gain knowledge	• Networking
• Attract new sponsors	• Get licensed	• Personal Growth
• Boost morale	• Improve skills	• Play
• Celebrations	• Increase membership	• Promote a new product
• Communicate issues	• Increase sales	• Public relations
• Education	• Job requirement	• Raise money
• Entertainment/fun	• Just because	• Recognition
• Exchange ideas	• Make decisions	• Solve problems
		• Support a cause
		• Training

IDENTIFYING YOUR PARTICIPANTS

When targeting people in a specific profession, age group, or gender, finding your participants is straightforward; but if they are from a variety of groups or from different areas, research may be necessary to find them. You will address this issue when you develop your defined vision. (See *Defining Your Vision*.)

Participants who attend events are members of associations or people with shared interests or a common cause. They are members of professional organizations, social clubs, fellow sports enthusiasts, members of special interest groups, bridge club, yacht club, or family members.

If size is not important, you may not need to search hard to find your audience. If your goal is large attendance, finding your potential audience will require compiling mailing lists from many different sources and using multiple media efforts to get them to your event.

LOCATION OPTIONS

As in business and real estate, location is a key factor in the success of an event. You want to match the location to the style of your event, to your audience, your theme, and your vision. The location should fit the occasion and be accessible for the majority of your guests. We thoroughly discuss how you select a location in the *Getting Specific in Your Design* section. Remember, you are not limited to the standards such as hotels, convention centers, or restaurants. Here is a partial list of meeting places to spur your thinking. ***Do not limit your imagination and be creative!***

LOCATION OPTIONS		
• Airport hotels	• Community centers	• Parking lots
• Airport hangers	• Conference centers	• Race tracks
• Amusement parks		• Resorts
• Aquariums	• Cruise ships	• Restaurants
• Arenas	• Downtown hotels	• Retreat centers
• Armories	• Downtown streets/square	• Skating rinks
• Art galleries		• Sports facility
• Atriums	• Dude ranches	• Tennis courts
• Backyards	• Fairgrounds	• Art Theaters
• Beaches	• Gardens	• Town halls
• Boat charters	• Golf or country clubs	• Warehouses
• Churches/ chapels synagogues/ temples	• Libraries	• Wineries
	• Mansions	• Yachts or yacht club
• Coliseums	• Mountain tops	• Zoos
• Colleges/ Universities	• Museums	
	• Parks/ campgrounds	

FUNDAMENTAL ELEMENTS OF EVENTS

The following common elements will be found in nearly every event you coordinate.

FUNDAMENTAL ELEMENTS OF EVENTS	
Vision	The main reason and focus for having the event, a combination of the goals and objectives.
Goals and Objectives	Every event will have goals and objectives whether they are set, discussed, and confirmed up front. Larger events might have several goals and objectives; each will be discussed and defined. For smaller or intimate events such as an anniversary party for your parents, the goals and objectives will be more obvious.
Site Selection	Location! Every event needs a site! It might be your backyard or an arena. It could be your local town hall, social club building, or a mansion.
Promotion	You must get your message out. The message could be as simple as the date, time, location, and reason communicated by telephone for a surprise birthday party. It could be as complicated as material for a week-long convention with numerous workshops, special events, outside excursions, banquets, and required registration information. Delivering this amount of information can take a multi-page brochure. It may require a quarter-page ad in your local newspaper, or a full page ad in *The New York Times* with a Web site sophisticated enough for online registration.
Participants/ Attendees	Without them, you would not have an event. Whether they are invited guests, paying participants, or required to attend, people will be coming to your event.

FUNDAMENTAL ELEMENTS OF EVENTS	
Agenda	This is a detailed outline with times of the activities. It logs what is happening from hours before the participants arrive to the follow-up when the event is complete? It is a schedule of what is happening throughout the event. There are two types of agendas to tell people where to be and what to do: one for the participants and the one for the people who work behind the scenes of the event.
Budget	We realize that with some events, no money will be coming in, such as a wedding or company social. You can create a budget anyway to track the amount being spent. For larger events, budgets are a must, especially when profit is one of your objectives. Without a budget it is hard to set guidelines and measure results.
Timeline	Whether it is written down or planned, every event has a beginning and ending time.
Food and Beverage	Food and beverage are always part of your event even when it is a short seminar with a pitcher of water and mints. But more often you will be planning a for larger amounts such as 10,000 attending a sit down dinner, an all-day concert where vendors serve the public, the morning sales meeting with coffee and doughnuts, an afternoon conference with soda and cookies, a three-hour cocktail party for 700 people with appetizers.

FUNDAMENTAL ELEMENTS OF EVENTS	
Transportation	You may need to transport 800 people to and from 10 hotels to the meeting site, or you only need get yourself to the site on time. You may need to arrange travel needs for entertainment, speakers, and VIPs including picking them up at the airport, or you may need to contract with an airline for discount airfare or negotiate with rental car companies for special rates for your participants.
Staffing	This could range from your checking in your participants for your workshop, or 100s of volunteers at a conference or sporting event. It could be the caterers, musicians, florists, cleanup crew, equipment setup, valets, ticket takers, MCs, speakers, or the balloon clown.

THE JOB OF THE EVENT PLANNER

Event planning is a process that starts by delineating the beginning and the end of the event. At that point it becomes a project and you are the project manager! It is not like your typical job where you go in and do the same thing every day. Your tasks and responsibilities change each day during the process and will be different with each event.

What are some of the things you think event organizers do? The job of the planner varies according to the size, scope, and complexity of the event. You may be asked to do any number of different tasks, including client consultation, setting budgets, choosing dates, selecting and inspecting a location, negotiating with and choosing suppliers, arranging transportation, booking blocks of hotel rooms, arranging catering, booking entertainment or speakers, writing copy for publicity, gathering leads for potential participants, choosing printers, creating an agenda, compiling participants' packets, gathering and directing volunteers, sticking on labels, or shipping boxes and that is all before the event day begins.

Each event is complex, diverse, and filled with unique characteristics. There can be thousands of details associated with one event. You will wear many hats, juggle a number of tasks simultaneously, and use many skills. One day you may be talking with a hotel and negotiating room rates, the next you are working on the budget, and later that afternoon you are writing copy for a brochure. Another day you may be entering names into a database and the next stuffing envelopes or flying off to do a site inspection. You will be interacting with CEOs, general managers, owners of a bed and breakfast, waiters, house cleaners, and everyone in between. You will meet or talk to different people every day.

With such a diverse range of events, often one coordinator is not enough. Choosing two or three competent people to have specific responsibilities can reduce stress and induce a successful event. Deciding how many planners are required should be addressed during the planning session.

CHOOSE YOUR ENVIRONMENTAL STANDARDS

One of the focal points in this guide is to help you as an event planner become more environmentally conscious of each decision you make. From the beginning of your planning process, think green. Before you know it, at every decision-making point you will consider the best alternative from an ecological and environmental mindset. There is a full chapter dedicated to ideas, options, and guidelines to help steer you in a new and sustainable direction. Environmental protection is not just a trend or a fad; it will soon become a requirement and eventually the normal way of doing business. We suggest you get a head start!

The Big Picture

Defining Your Vision

Being focused from the beginning is extremely important. Define what you want to achieve, what your vision encompasses, and commit your intentions to paper. You do this by defining your goals and objectives, setting your financial goals, and identifying your participants. You begin to envision how the event will look and feel. These points form the framework of an event that will be fleshed out right up till the end.

Your "defined vision" outlines everything that you do from this point forward. All the marketing material, each agenda, speakers or entertainment, and location will be based on and relate to your defined vision. In this chapter we will begin the developing stages and help you clearly define your vision and weave it into the final product.

The most efficient and effective way to create your defined vision is to hold a planning session with your staff or client and begin generating attainable goals and measurable objectives. After the vision is determined, create committees, assign roles, responsibilities, and tasks. Determine whether you need to hire outside consultants, vendors, and suppliers during these sessions. Outsourcing some responsibilities and tasks may be necessary to save you time and money.

During this meeting or at a subsequent meeting develop your financial goals. Decide if the event will be a for-profit event, and if so, how much will we need to charge? If not for-profit, how will we measure our return on investment? You need to know what your break-even point is and how to go about attaining it. If it is not-for-profit, pinpoint the source of the money. These questions and more will be determined in your planning sessions. (See more about financial goals in *Where is the Money?*)

We recommend that you create timelines and checklists before the event and amend them during and after planning sessions. The *Appendix* and **the companion CD-ROM** have samples of these forms for most areas of the planning process. Use these important tools to help remember the smallest details. Sometimes the smallest details really make the event.

All events are a process. Time spent in planning, writing, and designing your event in the early stages will result in increased attendance, repeat business, more publicity, and more money or all the above (or whatever your goals and objectives are).

No event is too small for an official planning session. Even if you are the only one attending the meeting, you still need to cover all of the basics: who, what, when, where, and why. No event is planned without answering these questions.

SETTING YOUR GOALS AND OBJECTIVES

Each event should have a goal and an objective to form the vision because without goals and objectives, you have no defined vision. We define goals and objectives as follows:

Goal — The general purpose of the event that provides a road map for the planning process.

Objective — A measurable, attainable target that contributes to the accomplishment of the goal.

An event can have one or many goals and typically multiple objectives supporting the goals. Call them what you like, but setting goals and objectives is necessary for successful events. Just do it — and do it early!

Companies, organizations, charities, and people in general produce events for many reasons, and there are thousands who attend and participate in them. There should be more than one purpose for your event. For example, you may want education to be the defined vision but you would also like to raise money, gain publicity, and have fun.

The partial list below shows some more examples of potential goals and objectives. Your participants often want or require one or more reasons to come to your event.

POSSIBLE GOALS AND OBJECTIVES		
• Accreditation/ certification	• Have fun	• Make a profit
• Attract members	• Improve skills	• Motivate
• Celebrate	• Incentive enhancing	• Network
• Come to a decision	• Inform	• Professional advancement
• Conduct business	• Inspire	• Recreation
• Develop	• Introduce like-minded people	• Reward
• Display	• Introduce new officers or board members	• Share and exchange information
• Educate	• Introduce new product or policy	• Solve problems
• Gain knowledge	• Improvement	• Support
• Entertain	• Learn something new	• Train
• Explore		
• Gain publicity		

SETTING FINANCIAL GOALS

Financial goals reflect your defined vision and the decisions you make regarding the return on your investment. You will want to establish your financial goals before creating your budget. It is similar to defining your goals and objectives before defining the type of event to produce.

Financial goals should fit into your overall goals and objectives. Your goal may be goodwill, promotion of a product, or something that will not have a monetary bottom line. However, a great number of events are produced for the sole purpose of making money. It is recommended that you set your financial goals early in the planning stages if profit is your purpose. With financial goals set, you can create your budget, price the registration/ticket fee, choose the location, and make decisions on the other costly aspects.

Return on Investment (ROI)

There are many ways to evaluate and measure the return on investment (ROI). It is not just about money; your objective may be profit, goodwill, or a testament of gratitude! It might have to do with the future of your business by training your sales team on new techniques or increase productivity by introducing new technology or giving motivational incentives. Whatever the financial goals or objectives are, they must have significance and be part of your defined vision. If it is profit that you are after, your ROI is calculated by simply dividing your net profit by your total costs and the result is the percentage of financial gain. Each and every event will have its unique return on investment.

Internal ROI

If it is goodwill you seek or the demonstration of thanks, you have to use other measures of success. They may be the large smile of the CEO as you present him or her a fabulous parting gift, witnessing the excitement of new members as they join the organization, recognition for a job well done, honoring the top sales force with incentive travel packages, getting publicity in the local newspaper, or simply to honoring a long time employee.

When it is profit you want, establish a solid budget and implement a measuring tool that will meet your objectives. If a sales increase is your goal, your annual sales report would be your measuring tool. If new members are your goal, then your membership records would be your tool.

External ROI

The ROI can be aimed at your participants, guests, and attendees. When that is the case, measuring success is difficult. One way of collecting information is through evaluation forms, receipt of thank you notes, an increase in enrollment, higher donations, more volunteers, or the bottom line.

Regardless of what your ROI is all about, it must be important to you and your organization, your clients and sales force, your family or peers, or whoever is the beneficiary of the event.

IDENTIFY YOUR POTENTIAL PARTICIPANTS

Whatever type of event you plan, it is for your participants. Who are they? Identifying and reaching the right people or group is crucial. It is about identifying those groups who will <u>want</u> to come to your event. It is about identifying those whom <u>you want</u> to attend your event!

Doing some extensive research is recommended if you question who your target market might be. You may want to survey potential attendees for insight into their needs, wants, and requirements. After all, they will know what is current in their field and what is important to know. If it is an annual event, use past participants to gather the data. Although most answers come from planning sessions, send out a survey to a portion of your database. Who are they? Here are a few possibilities:

POTENTIAL PARTICIPANTS		
• Association members • General public • Like-minded people • Women/men/both • Specific age group	• Certain income bracket • Similar ethnic backgrounds • Religious or spiritual groups • Technical, business related	• Family members • Fellow workers • Church group • Similar interests

Start a list of your target audience right now. Add to it as you move along in the process.

Your target audience may be your company's employees. However, there may be dozens of departments and different levels of management that are part of your target. Even though you know exactly where they are, you will still need to do some research to reach them.

If you are planning an all-day seminar for meeting planners, where will these participants come from? You can buy a list, create them from contacts and networking, or advertise for them. Do your research. Once you know who and where they are, attracting them is the next step. (See the section, *Marketing Your Event*.)

The Planning Sessions

Planning sessions should include all the significant players, those people who will be involved in the entire process: your staff, hired consultants, vendors, and accounting department. If they cannot attend the planning session, make sure they get the notes and summary report. If there is more than one meeting, continue to pass on the notes and reports. The decisions made in this meeting will be created, refined, confirmed, and even transformed with time, but these sessions will set the stage and create the foundation of the event. Roles and responsibilities will be established, and your target audience should be addressed and recognized. Use this time to establish the key decision makers, the core planners, your internal resources, and decide whether outside help is necessary.

We emphasize the importance of the planning sessions. The decisions you make will be based on one or more of your goals and objectives. The sessions furnish insight in making all of your future decisions with purpose and intention. You will set goals and objectives, begin designing your event, identifying and understanding your target audience, as well as set dates, times, and themes. This process might be frustrating at times, but if you get it right from the start, you will benefit by enjoying a smooth, well run event with great results.

These pre-event meetings are critical for the success of your event and will help to alleviate misunderstandings, create a cooperative atmosphere, and help you proceed with focus and clarity.

When the meeting concludes, write a summary of the decisions and distribute it to the appropriate people so that those who did not attend can pick up the file and carry on the process if for some reason, you, the planner, have to drop out.

If this is a repeat event, go over the final report from past events including the participants' evaluation summaries and the event planners' notes with improvement strategies. These historical notes can save you much time, frustration, and money. Do not reinvent the wheel, but be sure to improve upon and even make some drastic changes if necessary, especially if the old ways are obsolete. Some events with a long history will be a challenge to blend tradition and innovation. It will be your job to keep the tradition of the event as well as being relevant and contemporary.

A full day of planning is suggested for larger events, preferably two days if time allows, or they can be broken into smaller meetings over many days. Have these meetings periodically to report status and changes. It might be a good idea to have a "management retreat" at the same time as an intensive decision-making meeting. This is a critical time for delineating what you have to offer from what outside help is needed to put on an extraordinary show!

DESIGNING THE SESSION

Decide the framework for generating your first planning session(s). Answer these questions and add to the specifications as needed.

- Who should attend?

- Who will run the meeting?

- How many meetings are needed?

- How long for each meeting?

- Who will create the agenda?

- What goals and objectives will be discussed and determined?

- Who, what, when, where and why — logistics?

- Who gets the summary, reports, and notes?

- Where will the meeting be held?

What do you do first? Think big picture. What goals do you want to achieve? They should be strategic in nature, setting the stage for creating objectives to support them. If the question is "Why have the event?" the answer is in your goals.

Bring the following questions to the meeting to get your creative juices flowing for consideration on your goals and objectives:

POSSIBLE GOAL QUESTIONS – HIGH LEVEL

- What is your event's primary emphasis, the overall vision? Is it education, fun, product release, fundraising, anniversary celebration?

- Will this event be for the participants or for the organization? Who is the beneficiary?

- How important is financial success? Is our main focus profit, benevolence, or public relations?

- What information will you be sharing? (Will it introduce something new: a sales strategy, product line, CD, fundraising strategy?)

- What location is best? Where are most of our participants located, will they travel, do we need a popular destination, is money an issue for those coming?

- What is the target date? (Is it determined by the month, season, year, or day of week?)

- Who is your target audience? Are they our employees, family, club members, sales team, like minded people, industry groups, or students?

- Why do they want to attend? Is it education, fun, entertainment, interest, job requirement?

- Is the event required attendance or will they be paying?

- Can they afford to attend? Who will pay for their registration, travel, lodging, and other expenses?

- What is your budget? Is this a rate-conscious group? Are we making a profit?

- What kind of space is required? (Is it luxury, business, economy, fun, or adventure?)

- Will we need sponsors? Do we need to find additional funding?

POSSIBLE GOAL QUESTIONS – HIGH LEVEL

- Is this a repeat event? If so, what were the results of the last event? Are there past data? What do we need to do differently?

- Are the attendees repeats? Did they attend our past events? What evaluations were received?

- Is networking an important component?

- Are exhibits a component, either as a source of revenue or information?

- Will there be off-site events?

- How does environmental planning contribute to all of our decisions?

Below are a few samples of measurable objectives. Often more than one objective will be appropriate for each event.

Samples of measurable objectives.

- Increase sales by 20 percent.

- Teach participants about a new product.

- Provide training to sales staff.

- Define roles and responsibilities for the new planning committee.

- Roll out a new marketing program.

- Bring the family together for a celebration.

- Recruit 50 new members.

- Network with five new companies in similar business.

- Introduce 50,000 people to new software.

- Sell 500 "how-to" tapes and teach 1,000 people how to buy real estate.

- Earn a profit of $75,000.

- Sell 10,000 CDs.

- Introduce new board of directors.

- Raise money for political candidate.

- Announce new product to public.

- Celebrate partner Katie's birthday.

~ *Candy's Tips on Meetings* ~

Everyone involved in the event must communicate regularly: that means having meetings. Nine or ten months out, a monthly meeting is fine, but as the big date approaches, go to bi-weekly or weekly to make sure no one drops the ball and everyone has up-to-date information.

It is vital that good notes be taken at these meetings. People will forget they volunteered (or refused), dates might be confused, and the minutes may end up being a real life-saver. If these records or minutes are lengthy, do not waste time reading them at each meeting. Get them copied, mail them out in advance of the meeting, and ask for corrections before meeting time – excluding typos and spelling errors.

Money Saving Tips

- Have a good established agenda for planning session. Do not waste people's valuable time.

- Have available all past documentation that will be used and discussed.

- Have complete agenda prepared.

- Use local hotel space for meeting if off-site is necessary.

TIME FRAME FOR MEETING

Give yourself plenty of time for planning every aspect of the event. You will be surprised how much time certain tasks require, be it designing, writing, and editing marketing material, creating lists, mailing, finding the right caterer, or choosing a menu. For instance, venues typically need to be booked sometimes years ahead of time and really popular or well-known speakers and entertainers fill their calendars months or years in advance.

Sometimes you can pull off a large event in a short time but there is usually a price to pay—and not just money. You may not get the venue you want, the participants you need, the right speaker or entertainer. You may have to go second-class or take second-best or end up using leftovers. It is best to give yourself plenty of buffer time to coordinate your event. It is far easier to be early in planning than too late. One of the biggest reasons for a failed event is misjudging the timing.

ROLES AND RESPONSIBILITIES

Assign roles and responsibilities early in the process. There are many areas to cover, details to attend to, decisions to be made, and someone needs to do them. Who? Recognize when outsourcing (using outside vendors) is necessary. You may be a one-person show with all the decision-making power, such as putting on a one-day workshop for yourself. You are it! Or you could work for a large corporation like Birkenstock where you are one of many planners and decision makers. You may be the event planner for a resort, in which case the boss is the final decision maker, but you are also a decision maker in some areas. The scenarios are endless. Some questions need to be addressed, and roles and responsibilities need to be defined and confirmed.

You may be the chief, but if you are part of a larger corporation or association or one of several people working together, breaking up the duties can be extremely helpful. If the event is large, you might want to break down the roles and responsibilities in the following manner. This breakdown can be useful also when the event is smaller to keep your staff from getting in each other's way.

Key areas/teams at a very high level: remember, you may be a one-person team.

- **Operational** – This team has the overall responsibility of operations of the event, including management of all team members.

- **Financial** – This team determines sources of revenue, creates budgets and financial timelines, and designs the accounting systems.

- **Marketing** – This team knows the audience, promotional techniques, how to reach participants, how to design and implement the process, and understands the latest technology strategies.

- **Legal** – This team is clear on contracts, insurance, taxes, and is skilled at negotiations.

Assigning Roles and Responsibility

Roles and responsibilities will vary depending on the variables of your event. There are thousands of little jobs. Who is going to do them? Some tasks can be assigned right away and others can be assigned as coordination moves forward.

You may be responsible for logistics only and others responsible for writing and designing marketing materials while someone else is responsible for creating the agenda, obtaining permits, and even someone different may handle financial tasks. Be clear about who is doing what? Most important, know who can make financial decisions and who has the last say. Here are some of the questions, suggestions, and issues that need to be discussed:

- Who is the head coordinator?

- Determine decision-making chain of command.

- How many committees are needed?

- Who is in charge of each committee?

- How often should they meet?

- Divide areas of responsibility: program committee, logistics, budgeting, and promotions.

- Create checklists with appropriate details.

- Create schedules with achievable dates.

- After a committee's job is complete, place the members on another committee.

- Assign specific tasks to those responsible. When setting up committees try to match skills and talents with responsibilities.

~ Candy's Tips on Assigning Roles and Responsibilities ~

Should your event be so successful that it becomes an annual thing, congratulations! Now you have another potential problem: burnout! If the same person is in charge of the same portion of the event for three years in a row, I suggest that an assistant be assigned so that they can take over the job the following year. This is important because 1) it will take some of the load off the veteran and 2) it is a perfect training opportunity for the future planner to get him or her up to speed before taking over.

Some people are too proud to accept help, thinking that it makes them look incompetent. This way they will get assistance automatically, without feeling inadequate. If your event is really successful, they will need all the help they can get anyway.

CREATING TIMELINES AND CHECKLISTS

Do not underestimate the value of timelines and checklists. Just like every component in the event planning process, timelines and checklists will vary depending on your unique circumstances. These tools keep everyone involved on track and help you meet your deadlines! If you want to meet your deadlines, refine your timelines and checklists and use them often! See the sample checklists and timelines in the Appendix section. Amend these samples to reflect your specific event.

Timelines

When creating your timeline take these questions into consideration:

- Who is it for? The planner, the staff, the committees or all of these?

- Who should create them?

- How many are needed?

- Who is the keeper?

- How often will they be revised? Daily, weekly, monthly?

- Should you use software application to help manage?

- When to begin creating the timeline?

- Are the dates attainable and reasonable?

You can create your timelines with high level key dates or milestones only or you can be incredibly detailed with each task and deadline listed. It is your choice. Timelines are used to meet critical dates. A detailed timeline will ensure that no task or detail goes undone. Use the timeline that works best according to your event. We suggest creating several timelines for different areas of responsibility.

The best time to create a timeline is either during or after the planning session, after the dates are confirmed, after your site has been confirmed, or whenever you see appropriate. Remember the purpose of the timeline is to keep you on track; therefore, start early and keep it amended!

One way to create a timeline is to start from the day of the event and work backward. It may seem strange at first, but it works! Remember revise your timeline as often as needed. The point is to get everything down and give yourself enough time to complete each task.

Checklists

Similar to the timeline, checklists will vary depending on circumstances. They will keep you and everyone else moving steadily without omitting any details. Refer to your checklists often. The smallest missed task can ruin your day and throw off your schedule. If a task is written down, the chances of doing that task increases dramatically. Get it down on paper.

When is the best time to create checklists? How about starting right NOW! Create checklists during or after the planning session, after dates are confirmed, when roles and responsibilities have been defined, or whenever it is appropriate for you. The purpose of the checklist is to organize all the details. Be smart and start early!

As you develop your checklist include as much detail as possible for each task. For example, for the day of the event assign these types of tasks:

- Set up briefing with volunteers and staff

- Arrange for airport pickup for VIPs, speakers, and entertainment

- Assign supervisor for A-V equipment

- Find greeter

- Get help desk personnel

- Assign supervisor for breaks

- Assign supervisor for meeting room set-up

- Hang signs

- Meet with facility personnel

- Make sure to have cash on hand

- Have revised participants list

Refer to and use the sample timelines and checklists in the Appendix. Edit them to fit your particular circumstances. We expect that you will build upon them since they are samples only and will not cover all the details for your event.

Outsourcing

Outsourcing is hiring professionals outside your company who are experts in a particular field, such as a temp service to staff your registration table, your florist, security or audio-visual specialist, vendors, suppliers, marketers, designers, trades people, and consultants. In the planning sessions decide whether you need outside help and can afford it. Seasoned planners know when to use professional services for a variety of jobs.

Outsourcing will save time, money, and frustration. Consider hiring an expert to do the job if there is funding for outside help whenever a task is beyond your skills or experience, or you lack personnel or time. Even hiring an independent meeting planner can save you money.

When you decide to use outside assistance, create a partnership with the person or firm. Share the responsibility and commit to open and continuing communication. Pass on the most descriptive and detailed job description that you can. Bidders will want to know their responsibilities from the beginning. Of course, their duties may change slightly as the clock ticks down to the last minute. Pick someone who can grasp your vision and agrees with the culture of your business and the level of service you expect to provide. Succinct directions are important to this person. You may want to create a request for proposal (RFP) when searching for this person.

Examples of services you may need to outsource:

OUTSOURCING OPTIONS		
• Advertising/ Publicity/Public Relations • Airline and travel agencies • A-V technology companies • Balloon makers • Caterers • Convention and visitors bureau (CVB) • Copying services/ printing	• Destination management company (DMC) • Entertainment/ staging company • Equipment rental • Florists/ decorations • Graphic designer • Ground transportation • Hospitality greeters • Interpreters • Linens	• Mailing house • Marketing • Meeting facility • Publishing • Registration company • Security companies • Speakers bureaus • Travel directories • Temporary workers • Tent rentals • Web designers

For outdoor events, several services and vendors must be put under contract: a hotdog vendor, cotton candy and snow cone maker for a fair or party; a caterer, tent company, security team, buses, and valet attendants for other types of events. Sporting events have dozens of vendors responsible for tasks such as parking, security, food, T-shirt sales, or registrations. If possible, get references before hiring and signing any contracts. Use vendors who have a track record or were recommended by someone you trust.

If your event is in a town other than where you live, contact the local convention and visitors bureaus (CVBs) or check out local destination management companies (DMCs), and communicate with other event planners for suggestions and recommendations. See *Getting Specific in Your Design* for more detailed information on DMCs and CVBs.

Where is the Money?

*I*t is time to manifest the financial goals determined in the planning session. To implement the financial process, begin by creating your budget. A budget is a written document forecasting the potential costs and income of the event. It is a great monitoring tool to keep check on your spending. A well-created and maintained budget is an essential tool to allow you to project and supervise income and expenses, track cash flow, and verify how well you are doing at any given time. It will serve as your money guide throughout the planning process. You will refer to it often and will edit and update frequently.

The budget is incredibly important for many reasons. A realistic budget in the beginning will determine whether to take on the event. It will facilitate the decision-making process from start to finish and is a critical tool to help you spend your money wisely. It will also create the numbers for the formulas needed to find your break-even point and return on investment.

To have an accurate budget, you must know the source, arrival date, and amount of money that will be coming in. Identify your revenue and income so that you can plan when and how to spend it. Every expense goes into the budget. As you continue the process of planning your event and encounter more expenses, immediately put them into your budget.

Use historical data if available. Go over past budgets and see where you can either tighten or have room to expand your services. Take into consideration expense versus income and determine whether your registration fee or ticket price was too inexpensive or too pricey for your intended audience. Compare what you projected as opposed to the actual expenses. Note the most significant miscalculations. If this is a first-time event, you can begin with a zero base budget to be built on estimated expenditures and income.

Always take your defined vision into consideration when creating line items for your budget. You may desire fine wines, exotic flowers, exquisite food, and a venue with a breathtaking view but end up with taped music, simple decorations, and paper plates because you ran out of money. You decide where to spend your money. If your defined vision is to honor and impress the new board of directors, you will fail with paper plates. Your budget will keep you from making mistakes in spending and assist you in making educated decisions.

This is also a good time to determine who has authority for spending, who is responsible for maintaining the budget, how often it needs to be updated, and how the accounting should be done.

Determine early on where the money will be coming from and how much you will need. There are four sources of the money: your own reserves, sponsorship, participants, or a combination. Sponsors may make product donations that will offset your cash outflow. If the source is your participants, take into consideration that a large percent of the money will be spent before money will be coming back your way.

When expenses and income have been placed in the budget, find your break-even point and determine what style of accounting is appropriate for your event.

CREATING A BUDGET

As you begin to plan your event, laying out your proposed budget on a cost sheet will allow you to see what items can be included while staying within your budget. Watching the spending activity gives you the opportunity to use alternative options if the budget becomes over-extended. Should you find extra money, you may be able to add frills to the event or find a large profit coming your way.

Each event requires different expenditures so that there is no set formula or format for the budget. Walk though the event and write down all costs, taking everything into consideration. Revise the numbers as you get estimates and actual costs. Suppliers are happy to furnish you with written estimates for many of the expensive items your event will require. Get as many estimates as you can while you build your budget. The more accurate the numbers are in the beginning, the better the bottom line will be at the end. You can have a list of wish items to go into the event if money is available.

REVENUE/INCOME

Revenue can come to you in a variety of ways: contributions, registration fees, sponsorship, sales (T-shirts, books, audio tapes, or advertising space), franchise fees, exhibit space, or ticket sales. If you have a private individual writing a check to cover costs, consider yourself lucky. Not every event will generate income, but there must be a revenue stream to pay the bills.

SPONSORSHIP

Sponsorship is a common and widespread opportunity to fund an event. It is a great way to create a relationship or partnership with an organization or company that can last for years. It is a win-win situation for all concerned: the company gets name recognition and a direct line to their market. The event gets extra money, products, or donations to defray out-of-pocket costs, either in the form of cash or in-kind contributions. The participant gets information, product usage, information about the company and its products, and perhaps free gifts or product samples.

Companies no longer just sponsor an event for charity. Charitable intent might be part of the reason, but there are other motives behind sponsorship. Companies use these events as marketing vehicles to help them reach their customers. The times of sponsors' writing a large check, sending you their logos for promotional material, supplying products, and then walking away is over. Promotional tie-ins pop up in almost every aspect of today's events. Sponsorship is a direct way to build branding and product recognition to an audience, typically their customers, users, clients, and purchasers. A potential sponsor will want to reach large numbers of customers at one time. They can be creative in their marketing efforts with name on printed materials, signs, mementos, and hands-on usage at the event. Participants associated with a specific event (charity, environmental, political, philosophic, or cultural) can be allied with the product the sponsor wants to promote.

When looking for a sponsor, take into consideration how the participants and the products will match and if one is appropriate for the other. When you do partner with a sponsor, remember to give them VIP treatment and keep them in the loop as the event planning progresses.

> **Event: 10K walk**
>
> **Fundraiser charity**
>
> In one of my first sporting events I was the coordinator in charge of promotion and marketing. I had worked on several other events that had history and several solid sponsors. I was determined to find my own, and I did. Fortunately, many companies agreed that giving products was a great way to hit their target market. For one event, I was able to get fanny packs from a well-known sporting goods manufacturer, cases of a new soft drink, corn nuts, T-shirts, and coupons for hot tub use. I was delighted as were the participants of the event. Although there was no hard cash, the donations saved thousands of dollars in out-of-pocket expenses. The company that donated the soft drinks was so generous that we had twice the number of drinks as we had participants. We were able to save the remaining drinks for the following event.
>
> Shannon

EXPENSES

[handwritten: what can the ex Be·]

Expenses fall into three categories: fixed, indirect, and variable costs. Almost any fixed cost can turn into a variable cost if the meeting grows significantly or if you provide additional services or attractions. Likewise, variable expenses can turn into fixed expenses.

We have included an important list of expenses that many planners forget to figure into the budget. This list will help you create the most precise budget possible, but as always, something may slip through the cracks. Here is a brief description of the type of expenses you may encounter.

Fixed Costs

Fixed expenses are unchangeable regardless of sales or profits, nor are they adjusted based on the number of participants. Often they cannot be changed even when revenue falls short of expectations. A partial list of typical fixed expenses:

FIXED EXPENSES	
• Audio-visual equipment	• Meeting site/facility/venue
• Speakers	• Personnel salaries
• Insurance	• Entertainment
• Marketing and promotion	• Transportation
	• Signs

Variable Expenses

Variable expenses fluctuate based on the number of participants. You can calculate from the variable expenses just how much you will spend per person. A partial list of variable expenses:

VARIABLE EXPENSES	
• Accommodations	• Photography
• Additional site rental fees	• Placards
• Communications costs	• Power charges
• Decorations	• Promotional material
• Food and beverage	• Rehearsal costs
• Gifts	• Security
• Invitations/registration forms/ brochures	• Shipping, handling, and drayage
• Labor charges	• Signs
• Lighting	• Special effects
• Mailing	• Staffing
• Marketing and promotion	• Staging
• Menus	• Taxes
• Nametags/placards	• Transportation
• Office supplies	• Travel (to site inspection)
	• Wages for temporary staff

Events not held in a contained facility such as a hotel or convention center will require additional cost considerations. When the event is held outdoors in a park, at the fairgrounds, within the town plaza, or at the botanical garden, plan for the costs of these services in your budget. Some items to consider:

ADDITIONAL EXPENSES – OUTSIDE FACILITY	
• Alcohol sales/liquor permit • Catering • Cancellation fees • Glasses, dishes, silverware • Insurance – both you and contractors • Labor • Parking • Parking attendants • Permits • Power • Security	• Signs • Staff – maintenance, electrician, engineers, stagehands • Staging equipment • Tables and chairs • Tablecloths/skirting • Tents • Themes and decorations • Toilets • Traffic control • Waste/trash removal

On the next page is a list of expenses to be conscious about within a contained facility. Charges of this nature can be an unpleasant surprise on your final bill. Ask about these or other types of charges, fees, or tips. Negotiate these fees before signing the contract.

ADDITIONAL EXPENSES – CONTAINED FACILITY	
• A-V set up	• Internet access
• Attrition	• Meeting room setup
• Baggage handling	• Meeting room key
• Cleaning	• Mini-bar usage
• Computer	• Minimum bartender
• Copying	• Loading dock access
• Early departure	• Parking
• Easel rental	• Package delivery
• Electricians, maintenance, engineers	• Per-person minimum
• Energy surcharge	• Phone access
• Extension cord	• Resort
• Fax sending and receiving	• Room delivery
• Gratuity	• Safety-deposit box
• Hanging banners and signs	• Security
• Health club	• Storage
• Hotel shuttle	• Taxes

Discuss these fees and expenses with the venue before the event to eliminate any surprises charges on the final bill.

Indirect Costs

These costs are related to your organization's overhead. Administration costs, salaries, and office equipment.

Money Saving Tips

- Get bids for the major expenses and even some of the smaller ones. You will be surprised at the amount of money you can save by comparing bids for products and services.

- Create a simple spreadsheet with associated fees to calculate their impact on your meeting budget. If you are looking at comparing two cities, a difference of a few percentage points in taxes can make a big difference in the cost of your event.

- Are you tax exempt? Learn the rules for charities and non-profit companies. Can you be invoiced out-of-province or out-of-state and eliminate taxes there? What are the rules for charging tax on gratuities or services? Are you eligible for tax breaks that you are not claiming? A good tax consultant can answer these questions.

- Calculate your fixed, variable, and break-even costs. Know where your soft costs are and what is non-negotiable to your program, so that you have an idea of where you could spend less or what can be eliminated completely.

- Budget a 10 percent contingency to take care of unforeseen costs (for example, strikes or bad weather).

- Use volunteers when possible either from the community or your organization or club.

Breaking Even

If profit is your goal, you will need to know the break-even point. To get this measurement, a well-established budget is necessary. If your money is coming from registration, you need to know how many participants it takes to break even. If you know the number of participants, you will need to know how much to charge for registration or ticket sales.

How many participants are needed to break even?

Here is a sample calculation to find your break-even point. Add up your fixed costs and include site rental, speaker fees and expenses, and marketing costs. Let us use $75,000 fixed costs. Now add up your variable costs on a per person basis, including food and beverage, registration material, and shipping. Let us use $200 per person cost. Using a registration fee of $500 per person, deduct the variable costs. Divide the remaining amount into the fixed costs. Therefore, you would need 250 participants to break even. We used the following formula: Fixed costs ÷ (Registration fee – Variable costs) = number of required participants.

$$\$75,000 \div (\$500 - \$200) = 250$$

How to set registration or ticket fees to break even

If you have a good idea of the number of attendees or participants anticipated, you can find your break-even point and set your fees accordingly. You need to have your fixed and variable costs calculated using the confirmed number of participants. Add these two costs together and divide that number by your projected attendance. For example, using 250 participants, $200 variable expense and total fixed expenses of $75,000, you would need to charge $500 to break-even.

$$(\$75,000 + \$50,000) \div 250 \text{ participants} = \$500$$

Equipped with these numbers, you can determine whether you can make a profit. If the numbers do not work, here are some things you can do to change the financial dynamics:

- Increase attendance

- Increase registration fee

- Solicit sponsorship

- Reduce expenses

ACCOUNTING STYLES

Your accounting style should be based on your knowledge of event costs, availability of software, and the type of event you are producing. If your event is small, perhaps recording your expenses can be a matter of filing all of your receipts in a folder and entering numbers on an Excel spreadsheet. But the larger the event, the more important spending becomes, making proper recording practices is a must.

When your profit is your goal, then a more sophisticated system should be used. There are two popular accounting methods used in recording income and expenditures: cash accounting and accrual accounting.

Cash accounting is a simple and basic method and not really an up-to-date accounting of the big picture. It is basically recording your income and expenditures when they are received and when they are paid. Compare it your checkbook record. When a deposit is made, it is added to the accounting record. When a receipt is paid, it is entered into the recording device. This does not take into consideration any outstanding and known expenses yet to be paid or any outstanding income unpaid, but it may suit the purpose for your event. Do not make it more difficult than it need be.

The **accrual accounting** method is a little more complicated, but it is more accurate because it takes into consideration money that has yet to be spent or received. It accounts for committed income and expenses in the month that they are expected to be acquired or paid. In other words, accrual accounting shows money as income even though you have not received it and shows money debited even though it has not been paid out.

Keeping up with the spending activity is also very important for larger events. Review and update the accounting ledger and budget regularly during the course of the planning process.

Greening Your Event

Planning For the Environment

As event planners, you are in the perfect position to make a great contribution to the health and sustainability of the planet. You also have an opportunity to educate everyone involved in the event production industry. By changing the way you do business to green-up at every occasion, you can do a great deal to help our planet.

At any given moment there are thousands of meetings and events going on with millions of attendees traveling to and from different locales throughout the world. The events industry is perfectly situated to have an extraordinary environmental impact by making a few changes on a daily basis. Every change will make a difference.

Our industry encompasses so many other industries and businesses that any change we make has a wide influence. We can exert considerable pressure on transportation, food and beverage industries, hotels, convention centers, and hospitality businesses. Every aspect of doing our business can play a role in sound environmental causes. This is a powerful position to be in and we must take it seriously.

The population is ready to take on more responsibility as it becomes concerned with ecological issues. Changes you make will reflect the increasingly common worldwide use of the word "green" to cover everything from global warming to recycled paper.

The more you act responsibly, the more questions you ask, and the more knowledgeable you become, the greater the impact you will have. Use our resources wisely and leave a lighter footprint on our communities, our cities, and the planet. It is becoming popular to demonstrate social and environmental responsibility. It looks good for corporations and groups in general to be making "green" choices.

You may have to change your way of doing business as usual, but think of the rewards and the satisfaction you reap knowing that you have contributed to saving resources instead of depleting or wasting valuable natural products. It takes a little more effort to plan a green event or to do anything the unconventional way, but then again, you are event planners who are always up for the challenge, and being resourceful and creative is your hallmark.

Events and meetings create huge amounts of waste. One event can leave behind tons of waste—food, cardboard, handouts, paper, Styrofoam, and plastic. Most of that is not biodegradable and it is heading to our landfills. A few changes in one event alone can save trees, water, or carbons and keep tons of waste from hitting our landfills. Try small steps at first and see how easy it becomes after a while. You will feel so good about the results you will be eager to change another aspect of your business.

What is Green Planning?

Green planning is a responsible way of doing business that includes energy conservation, minimizing consumption of natural resources, reducing waste, recycling, and using earth-friendly products. Design the event by deliberately incorporating environmental plans in every stage of the process and to minimize any negative impact on the environment. From choosing your destination to deciding on what food to serve, each choice is made with this consideration.

Green meetings are not the mainstream yet, but they are evolving so that venues, suppliers, and participants are responding by following some of the green practices in this guide. Because the public and planners are starting to be green, many suppliers, especially hotels and convention facilities, are implementing more environmentally friendly processes and programs. The more you request and ultimately hire these services, the more suppliers and vendors will incorporate green practices too.

Whether you are an independent event planner or work for a company, you can develop and establish a baseline of criteria, policies, approaches, and guiding principles as your standard practice. Depending on your situation, you can use all or some of these standards. The first step is committing to making changes. The second is creating your standards and share them with everyone involved with the event, including your participants. Identify where you are willing to compromise since all standards will not be applicable at all times. Last, measure your results. You will be amazed at some of the facts and figures you realize.

THINK LOCALLY

One decision you can make right up front is to buy local and use locally made products. For example, if your event is in California, do not have Maine lobster flown in. Use locally caught salmon or crabs from the nearest coastal city. Do not fly in a speaker from Florida when there are qualified speakers in the city where you are hosting your event. If you are in Santa Fe, do not use flowers grown in Hawaii. Decorate your event with local cacti and create your theme around them. Using non-local goods means you are wasting fossil fuels to fly in the products, creating extra packaging waste and additional expense for freight and travel. Better yet, you are actually helping out that local community and their farmers, fishermen, artisans, craftspeople, and business people. You are helping to sustain their living. As for your guests, they benefit by experiencing the local flavor of the area and all the treasures it has to offer.

Even when your event is not local for you the planner, try to bring the flavor of your locale into the event by using the natural ambiance as your theme. You can actually save money by integrating the neighboring wares and goods into the food and décor to enhance your participants' experience and create a fond memory of the event.

Try specialty foods from the region or famous foods such as fresh crabs or oysters in San Francisco, halibut in Alaska, Texas beef barbecue in Houston, Boston Clam Chowder in New England, local lobster in Maine, or perhaps Hispanic food in Florida. You get the picture.

Use the local flora and fauna for decorations and appeal. Do not have cut flower bouquets on the tables but potted flowers that can be given to the guests or to local children's hospitals or retirement communities after the event. They are also perfect gifts or prizes for a raffle.

You can save on travel, hotel, and food costs by using local speakers and entertainers.

Instead of shipping everything to the out-of-town site, rent or buy locally. Think twice about having something specially made just for one event; try to have signs made that can be reused for multiple occasions. Typically any manufactured item will generate 70 times its weight of waste during manufacture.

IS A MEETING NECESSARY?

Another question that should be considered, is the meeting necessary? Do we need to do a face-to-face or will another method of sharing the information suffice? We know that face-to-face meetings and gathering groups of people will never cease, but there are times when bringing your entire sales force together is not the best use of time and money. With today's awesome technology, meetings via phone and computer may be adequate.

Online meetings and conference calls are becoming more popular as technology improves and energy prices rise. It is common for corporations and businesses to have their regular business meetings via phone or computer. Webinars, Web casting, video streaming, and teleseminars are a few of the more accepted and practical forms of meeting today, reducing travel, expenses, time, and waste of natural resources.

SETTING YOUR ENVIRONMENTAL STANDARDS

An important part of your responsibility as an event planner is making choices. Do you want chicken or beef? Shall we have a buffet or seated service? Will we have handouts or place the presentation on our Web site? What city is the best choice for this meeting? Shall we serve snacks at the breaks or just coffee? Paper or plastic? The decision making process is endless. Every choice you make will have an environmental impact. If you set your own environmental standards, you can easily make consistent choices by putting them into practice. You will know where and on what you are willing to compromise.

How committed are you to greening your events? This level of commitment will direct your standards. What are your criteria for a green event? What are your priorities? Develop a plan outlining your standards, your commitments, and your plans for implementing them. You will be able to use these guidelines when sending your request for proposal (RFP) to vendors, suppliers and venues.

Here are some of the most important areas that affect the environment. Take a look at each of these areas and see how you can incorporate a few or all of these into your event planning process. Look at each area below and set your standards accordingly.

Destination: Often the city has been chosen without your input, but if you have a say in the location, choosing a green destination city will make your green planning process much easier. If you are the one who selects the destination, choose a city that minimizes travel for participants and has everything you need locally. There are many ways you can transform any city to green your events. A few things to consider are listed on the next page.

- Ask the CVB or DMCs to find venues, vendors, and suppliers who meet your environmental standards. Ask for a list of green venues, properties, vendors, and suppliers.

- Look into the mass transit systems connecting the major venues with other transportation services.

- Is the city served by adequate airlines to allow for fewer flights and minimize layovers? If your destination requires extensive travel for participants, consider using "carbon offsetting" programs. (See Travel Ideas for further explanation.)

- Submit an RFP with your environmental standards.

- Is the city walkable? Are there nearby attractions?

Accommodations: Hotels and resorts have come a long way to improve their green practices. There is a wide variation in their environmental consciousness.

- Choose hotel and event venues that connect to the airport by mass transit and are within walking distance of one another.

- Ask venues for their in-house environmental policies and a description of the programs in place.

- Have hotels complete the checklist and detail their environmental performance. Give preference to those with the best scores.

- When doing a site visit, verify that your environmental standards will indeed be met.

- Choose a hotel that is willing to go with your standards.

Venue: Conference centers are also becoming more environmentally responsible. (See list in this chapter.) Here are tips to make sure your choice is a sound one and to encourage your venue to become greener.

- Choose a venue that is connected to the airport by mass transit and within walking distance of the hotel. Ask the hotel if they have van service.

- Request a copy of their environmental policy and plan.

- Find out what in-house environmental programs the venue offers.

- Perform a site visit to verify that your environmental service requirements can be met.

- Find out if the venue has had any environmental audits performed in the last five years. Ask to see the reports.

- Choose a venue that is willing to cooperate with your standards.

- Try to locate the hotel and meeting venue within walking distance of each other.

Transportation: One of the most significant environmental impacts of your meeting will result from how you move people around and how far they travel.

- Have those who cannot travel attend virtually by using new technology.

- Choose a destination with minimal travel requirements for participants.

- Communicate to the attendees the environmentally preferable transportation choices for getting to their destination. Commuter trains and other mass transit systems are preferable to car travel.

- If air travel is required, recommend an airline that has a sound environmental program.

- Make it easy for guests to get to the airport from the meeting venue. Provide information about the local public transit system or arrange for carpooling shuttles.

- Purchase electronic tickets for airline tickets.

- If traveling by car, look for vehicles that reduce emissions: electric and hybrid powered. Vehicles using natural gas, propane, methane gas, and ethanol are good options.

- Provide a public transit pass and map in delegates' packages.

- Establish a carbon-neutral initiative to counteract the CO_2 emissions from your event.

Food and Beverage: By working closely with your food and beverage supplier, you can make some small changes that have a big impact or big changes that have a grand environmental result.

- Ask that condiments, beverages, and other food items be provided in bulk instead of individually packaged. Do not serve water in individual plastic bottles.

- Ensure food and beverage packaging is recyclable and that it will be recycled.

- Give your delegates reusable coffee mugs at the start of the conference.

- Ask your supplier to buy local produce in season to avoid costly transportation of goods.

- Offer fair trade, shade grown, and organic coffee.

- Request organic produce and free range chicken/eggs/meats.

- Offer vegetarian meal selections; vegetables consume less land and energy to produce.

- Request participants to sign-up for meals. Letting you know how many meals they will be attending will reduce food waste and your costs.

- Have untouched food donated to a local food bank or soup kitchen.

- Ask that leftover food be composted or shipped to a local farm as livestock feed.

- Use reusable cutlery, dishware, and linens.

- Choose reusable centerpieces and decorations such as living plants or silk flowers. Give these away as table prizes.

Communications and Marketing: Your communications and marketing are a chance for you to make your environmental efforts known, and using new media and electronic delivery can also save you some money.

- Share your standards with all those involved: management, suppliers, participants, presenters, and exhibitors.

- Use the Web and e-mail to promote your event.

- Use electronic registration and publish the conference agenda on-line.

- When hard copy material is necessary, print on both sides and use soy or vegetable-based inks and recycled, chlorine-free paper.

- Ask your hotel to dedicate a TV channel to conference information and updates.

- Avoid paper duplication by giving participants their packages when they check in rather than before.

- Offer electronic proceedings of the events.

- Ask presenters to minimize paper hand-outs.

- Present speakers' notes electronically along with conference minutes.

- Use your leverage with your contracted services and encourage them to go green with their communications.

Exhibition Production: Including your exhibitors and facilities in your standards eliminates unnecessary waste.

- Create signs for reuse.

- Provide collection bins for recycling name tags.

Tell your exhibitors about your standards. Get them involved by asking them to:

- Print their materials on recycled paper and use vegetable-based inks.

- Bring only what is needed to the event and take away what they do not give out.

- Use items for the free handouts and trinkets that are made from recycled materials, durable or reusable.

- Promote their own environmental initiatives.

Bring the facility on board. Request that:

- Provided on-site recycling for paper, cans, glass, and other materials that are generated.

- They choose reusable decorations and display materials. Ask local schools, retirement facilities, or charitable organizations if they would like to receive used decorations after the event.

- Provide separate receptacles for recyclable and the garbage.

- Request that the display booths be created using recycled, reusable material.

10 EASY STEPS

Ideally the above steps are some great practices; however, many destinations, sites, hotels, venues, and caterers will not have the ability to fulfill your wish list. If you do nothing else, here are ten easy steps that everyone can take to lessen the impact of your event:

1. **Create your standards**. Establish your environmental standards in writing and get buy-in from the host organization's management. Share your standards with suppliers, vendors, speakers, and participants. You will be amazed at how far they will go to help.

2. **Use technology**. Use new media and electronic technology to cut down your paper needs. Create a conference Web site, offer electronic registration and confirmation, and advertise using the Web and e-mail.

3. **Choose a close destination**. Reduce distances traveled by speakers and participants. Choose a host city that is close to as many delegates as possible, and choose a venue and hotel that are near the airport and within walking distance of each other.

4. **Practice the three environmental Rs**. Ask your hotel or event venue to provide visible, accessible reduction, reuse, and recycling services for paper, metal, plastic, and glass.

5. **Bulk up**. Have your food and beverage provider use bulk dispensers for sugar, salt, pepper, cream, and other condiments.

6. **Use less**. Choose a hotel that offers a linen reuse program and bulk dispensers for shampoos and soaps in guest suites.

7. **Eat healthy**. Include vegetarian meals and have meals planned using local, seasonal produce and free range meats.

8. **When paper is necessary — close the loop**. Have all printed materials published on recycled paper, using vegetable-based inks, and printed on both sides of the page.

9. **Save energy**. Coordinate with the event venue to ensure that lights and air conditioning will be turned off when rooms are not in use.

10. **Share the news!** Tell participants, speakers, and the media about your success. You will be surprised. Green efforts are contagious.

TRAVEL IDEAS

There will always be travel of some kind in the meeting and event business, and thousands of participants, staff, speakers and entertainers will travel by airplane, car, bus, and even train. As we have said, the first step is to choose a convenient destination where fewer people travel long distances to get there.

To compensate for whatever travel does take place, buying carbon to replace emissions is the newest way to counter-balance negative impact from the travel. Carbon offsetting erases the impact of your trip by reducing carbon emissions somewhere in the world in proportion to the damage caused by your travels. For instance, it would cost about $5.50 to offset the carbon used for a round trip from San Francisco to Orlando for one person.

Organizations that can help reduce your carbon footprint and support climate-friendly projects are The Pacific Forest Trust, Climate Care, Carbon Fund, or Native Energy to name a few. Depending on where you make a donation, the money is used for conserving forests for their climate benefits, building wind farms in India and the United States, restoring the rainforest in Uganda, installing energy efficient lighting in South Africa, providing energy-efficient stoves in Madagascar, or funding a renewable farm methane project in the Midwest. When you buy a carbon offset, your money is used to fund projects that reduce emissions on your behalf. These are just a few organizations that are attempting to reduce emission. Do a search yourself on this issue to find others. We do not particularly promote any one organization over the other. We promote the concept!

How does carbon offsetting help fight global climate change?

Carbon offsets are an easy and cost effective way for any person or business to take action to stop global warming caused by the build-up of greenhouse gases in the atmosphere from human activity. It enables individuals and businesses to reduce their CO_2 emissions by displacing the CO_2 elsewhere, typically where it is more economical to do so. Carbon offsets include renewable energy, energy efficiency, forest protection, and reforestation projects. As more and more people are concerned about global warming and seek to reduce their climate impact, carbon offsets, along with personal carbon reductions, provide an important solution to global warming.

Carbon offset providers often provide a "carbon calculator" for individuals to estimate the carbon dioxide emissions arising from their consumption of electricity, gas, and air travel. You can suggest that participants look into making a donation; you can split the costs, or have a sponsor pick up the tab for the entire number of guests. You will be doing your part in reducing emissions on the planet.

Using carbon offsetting within your business can have benefits for you. It is a great public relations approach. You can demonstrate your responsiveness and willingness to make a global difference to your target market, clients, attendees, and colleagues.

Put in writing that you are donating to a fund or that your sponsor is donating. Use the information in the marketing material, the material provided at the event, on your Web site, and on signs at the event. If you do not want to pick up the entire tab, you can provide donation envelopes to your participants who can play a part if they want. If nothing else, it spreads the news. The changes would be dramatic if everyone contributed just a little to making a difference. There are many Web sites listed in the Resources section in the Appendix. Check out your calculations for your next event.

EVENT AWARDS AND CERTIFICATION

There are a couple of organizations that are certifying or awarding events that meet the criteria and measure up to being environmentally sound. This means planners must qualify and maintain a certain standard to be awarded and certified. The Green Meeting Industry Council together with IMEX and the International Hotels Environment Initiative gives awards to conferences that meet their standard of green events. One such certification organization is the Cleaner and Greener a Program of Leonardo Academy, Inc.

About the Green Meetings Award

The award recognizes environmental awareness among meeting organizers, highlighting opportunities to stage business tourism events in "green-minded" venues, while also planning an agenda that takes global warming issues into account.

Previous Winners

In 2006 the Green Meetings Gold Award was presented to the **U.S. Green Build International Conference and Expo 2004** (USGBC). Their strategy for its 2004 Green Build Conference was to enlist the help of convention centers, hotels, caterers, exhibitors, and decorators in minimizing waste by reducing consumption, pollution, and waste at source. Outcomes for the 2004 event included a saving of $25,000 through the use of water stations and compostable cups instead of water bottles. An audit measured waste output at the Oregon Convention Centre and the hotel and showed that 48 percent of solid waste was recycled while 23.9 percent of food served was composted. An additional 3,450 pounds of food were donated to a local community service organization.

The 2006 Silver Award winner, **the Sierra Club**, was praised for introducing clear contract measures and achieving excellent waste management reduction at its first ever four-day annual conference in San Francisco in September 2005 with 4,000 delegates.

The Boston-based **Coalition for Environmentally Responsible Conventions** (CERC) won the 2005 award. CERC was praised for its work during the 2004 Democratic and Republican political conventions in the United States. The organization was formed in 2004 by 15 local environmentalists in direct response to the Democratic Convention's being held in Boston. CERC also targeted the Republican Convention in New York in its efforts to increase awareness and improve overall environmental education among meeting planners throughout the United States. They make it easy to offset pollution caused by an event by calculating emissions from energy use and work with event organizers to reduce them. After the event, they recognized the event for the level of offsets achieved.

Cleaner and Greener calculates emissions caused by:

- Electricity and fuel use during the event

- Travel to and from the event

- Food preparation and cleanup for event meals

- Electricity used in hotel rooms

Reducing all types of emissions is important. The pollution caused by energy use includes carbon dioxide, particulate matter, nitrogen oxides, and sulfur dioxide. Each type of pollution causes its own particular set of environmental and health problems, so that offsetting all different types of pollution caused by energy use is important for environmental improvement.

Organizations that register their event with Cleaner and Greener Event Certification make a commitment to work with the program to gather emission use and to offset the emissions caused by energy use associated with their event. If you want to sign up to have your event certified, the group will help you to lessen the environmental impact of your event, provide you with copy for your marketing material and participants handouts, provide pre-and post-event emission statistics, and even assist in processing tax deductible donations.

BEYOND RECYCLING

Research shows that during a typical five-day conference, 2,500 attendees may use 62,500 plates, 87,500 napkins, 75,000 glasses or cups, and 90,000 bottles or cans. Is this something we have a say about? Absolutely!

Multiply those items by thousands of attendees and exhibitors and you can have several tons of waste produced from just one major event. The good news is that as meeting planners, you can find ways to reduce the waste produced at all of your events, large and small.

You can do something simple such as requesting that your participants recycle. Put the request in brochures and agendas; make announcements to remind people to recycle; have visible bins for cans, bottles, and paper; collect and reuse tote bags and name badges. These are very easy remedies to filling the landfills with unnecessary waste.

The next step in green thinking following recycling is to use alternatives. The emphasis is now on conserving our resources, efficiency in usage, reducing consumption, re-usage of products, and then recycling. Instead of plastic or paper plates that can be recycled, use glass or china dishes. Free yourself from having to recycle at all.

By using the following straightforward tactics one event with 23,000 participants and 100 exhibitors were able to recycle more than 26 tons of waste and achieve a waste diversion rate of 95 percent. It saved about 238 trees, 4,300 gallons of water, and nearly 30 cubic yards of landfill space. Now that is progress! The event planners worked in partnership with the venue to promote recycling, and they did the following few effortless changes to achieve the above outstanding environmental impact.

- Replaced the non-recyclable Styrofoam cups and plates with plastic or glass ones.

- Trained all staff appropriately and got them invested in the program and excited about the intentions.

- Installed customized three-bin separated waste containers for bottles and cans, paper, and organic waste at all concessions and food service locations.

- Supervised the docks to ensure departing exhibitors used the correct bin and knew what materials to take back home with them.

- Enlightened the participants and exhibitors ahead of time that recycling was an important aspect of the event. They placed recycling information in the registration materials, brochures, and agendas.

All of these strategies and more can be integrated into any event regardless of size, location, number of people, or vision. You can create this environmental atmosphere no matter what your event is all about.

Event: Jim and Nancy's Environmental Wedding

Venue: Outdoor public park

Participants: 150 guests

When we decided to marry, we carried our strong environmental beliefs into the planning of our wedding. Here are some of the changes we incorporated that gave our wedding a green theme.

Our announcements were eco-friendly invitations from a green company and they used the company's line of Grow-a-Note products. They were made from recycled paper printed with soy-based inks and embedded with a mixture of wildflower seeds. After the wedding, guests could plant the invitations in soil and watch flowers bloom. They were beautiful invitations.

At the celebration, we spent four hours eating and drinking. Four hours! We had the caterer use only locally grown vegetables and fresh caught fish, and, oh yes, a chocolate fountain for the children. We didn't want to be short on food and fun, but we just were conscious about what we chose to eat, drink, and how we decorated. Any leftover food went to the local homeless shelter, and the flowers were taken to the children's wing of the hospital.

We picked the flowers from our garden and asked the floral designer to enhance the arrangements with other local flowers. For those who traveled from out-of-town we asked them to contribute to an environmental friendly organization instead of a gift for us. After the honeymoon, we calculated the travel for our guests and our honeymoon and then wrote a check to The Pacific Forest Trust to balance out our impact.

It could have been easy enough to eliminate the environmental impact by eliminating the party, but that would prevent us from sharing our happiness with the people we love best. And that is certainly not the point. It is to celebrate joyfully but consciously.

Nancy K. C.
Sebastopol, CA

Sign of the Times

Studies show that socially and environmentally responsible companies are inclined to prefer a green venue over a traditional one. The problem today is that there are not that many choices. (See short list in the next section for green convention centers.) When you find a green venue, begin to work with the staff and then work with your participants to make the meeting green. There are many levels where you can request a change such as asking for recycled paper products to be used, cleaning solutions to be environmentally safe, no plastic or Styrofoam used during your stay, and recycling bins throughout the facility. You may teach them a green thing or two to put into practice.

When the property has a good reputation for green practices, it will attract like-minded organizations, environmental groups, conservation organizations, governmental entities, and educational groups to use that venue. As this trend gathers awareness and momentum, more and more groups will require environmental practices from their venues.

GREEN VENUES

When greening their facilities, properties save on operating costs, such as ongoing increases in energy charges that are crippling many facilities' profitability, making these efforts save planners money, too. The bonus is that most green practices over time do save money, making them worthwhile pursuits above and beyond the environmental impact and waste reduction and good public relations. The myth that applying green practices can cost considerable money is just that, a myth. Actually, savings are more likely.

Environmentally friendly cleaning products, recycling, and composting save money. Even the much-made-fun-of card in your hotel room that asks if you want your linen changed every day makes a difference. Economically Sound Company has an eco program called Green Suites International. In 2005 alone, their hotel clients collectively replaced some 250,000-plus lights with energy-efficient bulbs, saving more than 70 trillion kilowatt hours of electricity and avoiding 7 million tons of carbon dioxide emissions every year from coal fired power plants. They have implemented water-efficient guest room solutions such as sink aerators and low-flow shower heads, saving an estimated 250 million gallons of water per year. By installing more than 10,000 Guestat Energy Management Systems, they saved 10 trillion kilowatt hours of electricity and avoided 5 billion tons of carbon dioxide emissions every year. They added more than 14,000 bathroom amenity dispensers, annually diverting more than 10 million plastic bottles from landfills. In adopting a linen-and-towel reuse program, they conserved more than 100 million gallons of water a year.

There are several American convention and conference centers that currently identify themselves as green. Some are much more advanced in the environmental arena than others. Throughout the United States, cities are finding it important that when upgrading or building new convention centers, environmental concerns are on the top of their list.

Lawrence Convention Center in Pittsburg, Pennsylvania, is green by design. The facility's design and construction incorporate a variety of greening elements, including recycling up to 80 percent of waste and using non-toxic, recycled materials. As the United States' first green convention center and the world's largest green building, the center capitalized on its environmentally smart structure by using a water reclamation system, natural daylight, and natural ventilation for light and heat. All of the greening efforts were expected to cut the facility's utility costs by 40 percent, paying for the initial investment in seven to ten years.

The Hawaii Convention Center in Honolulu was also designed under a green program. The center saves tremendously in operations that ultimately drive costs down for planners and suppliers through energy efficiencies.

The recent expansion of the Oregon Convention Center in Portland was done with environmental concerns in mind. The most inspiring visible green feature is the "rain garden" that collects about 1,000 cubic feet of runoff (just under 7,500 gallons) from the five-acre roof and filters it through a bioswale. The garden is an attractive addition to the exterior, providing a picturesque fountain that returns water to city sewers cleaner than when it rained from the sky. The glass features a low e-coating to maximize light and minimize unwanted heat. This measure will reap energy savings of some 66,000 kilowatt hours. They even have an in-house "green team" to improve their environmental practices. Portland's light-rail system goes from the International Airport to the Convention Center. The City also has the FlexCar program for alternative transportation.

The Long Beach, California, Convention Center has newly installed solar power panels. An electric inverter, a transformer, and cables to go along with some 4,000 solar panels are being installed on the center's roof. It is expected to save thousands of dollars in energy costs.

The new convention center in Anchorage, Alaska, is using hi-tech to go nearly green. It has five hi-tech systems with energy management, and it is operated from remote computers to control the fire alarm and life safety, security, closed-circuit television, audio, heating, ventilating, and air conditioning systems. Operators can remotely turn off lights and turn down temperatures in empty rooms, and set the system up to be warm just before an event. The new center will employ a heat system that uses less outside air, bringing cost savings, especially in winter.

The Spokane Convention Center in Washington will be going green to promote a healthier environment. The developers are working to qualify the expanded 100,000-square-foot exhibit hall as an official green building.

The San Francisco Moscone Center offers a sustainability program where planners have the opportunity to recycle up to 70 percent of their waste. Their program recycles or donates cardboard, foam core, cans, bottles, paper, wood, metal, and even leftover carpet padding. Their in-house caterer uses china service instead of disposable wares, economizes on water, uses organic seasonal foods and wines, and composts all food waste. The administrators choose biodegradable packaging options for cutlery, lunch boxes, and salad bowls made from corn starch plastic.

SHARING YOUR RESULTS

If you were able to track your positive environmental and economic impact, publish the results. People love to hear success stories and especially ones in which they played a role. Therefore, notify, electronically of course, your participants, sponsors, clients, vendors, suppliers, and the media. Your report just might inspire all involved and perhaps enlighten them to the ease of practicing green standards in their everyday life. 🐬

High Level
Logistics

Getting Specific in Your Design

At this point you should have completed your defined vision, goals and objectives, financial goals, set your environmental standards, and begun work on the budget. You have the "why." Now it is time to get the "when, where, and how." With some of the major decisions concluded it is time to design your event by picking time and dates, destination and location, choosing your speakers and entertainers, and creating the agenda.

Do not take this section lightly. It will determine the success or failure of your event. Will you meet your goals and objectives? Will your participants walk away from this event satisfied that they got what they came for, and will they receive what you promised them? Will you make that return on investment that you planned for?

Everything you decide to do pertaining to this section will be used and reflected in creating your marketing and promotional materials. You will use this information to design your agendas; it will affect your budget, influence who your participants are, and touch every other detail regarding your event.

CHOOSING THE RIGHT DATES

Picking specific dates and times for your event is crucial to attracting participants to your event. Whether it is four days long or just two hours, it will start on a specific day at a specific time and end on a specific day at a specific time. You will want to do some research before selecting these specifics since they are central to your success. Be sure that similar events are not happening around the same time and double check that the dates will not interfere with your participants' other commitments. Can you imagine how many tax accountants would come to your event on April 10th? Avoid a conflict in dates with your intended audience whenever possible.

It might be ineffective to hold a 10-mile run in San Francisco the same weekend as the famous 100-year-old Bay to Breakers, or to plan a medical conference the same month as the annual American Medical Association Convention. You do not need the competition for participants. Pick dates when your attendees have an open calendar.

Usually the date is already established and non-negotiable. If so, you have to work around that date — not vice versa. Annual events often are the same day in the same week of the same month every year. A fixed date has advantages and disadvantages. If you wanted a specific venue but it was previously reserved for that time, you are out of luck. You cannot change the date to fit the venue.

Check all available sources for other events scheduled in the area. Talk with the convention bureaus in the area where you are holding your event. Peruse the Internet for dozens of topics related to your event and look for similar events going on either locally or nationally. Take into consideration major holidays, religious observations, school breaks, and extra long weekends. Do not overlap something that is already on the calendar of your potential participants.

Other thoughts to take into consideration when choosing the time and date for your events are: What days would be best? Would mid-week be better than a Thursday, Friday, or weekend? Where are your participants coming from? If people are traveling, take into consideration travel time, costs, and work schedules.

Early morning may be better to start your meeting if late afternoon traffic is a nightmare in your area. Fridays may be a hard day to keep your participants at the event and paying attention. By noon they may be planning an early escape to start the weekend.

For special events, midweek or Saturdays and nights draw the most people. Again ask a few questions. Will they be coming from work? Will they need to change their clothes before the event? What time do they get off work? Will traffic be an issue for the participants and volunteers? Will their partners be invited? Will they come in separate cars? Will there be enough parking?

Consider all the possible problems or issues that can hinder your participants' attendance and avoid as many as possible.

When picking a date for an athletic event called "Run from Your Taxes" we picked April 15th which fell on a Saturday. I thought how perfect, everyone would be done with their taxes and want to get outside for a fun run. I thought the registration form was clever. It was nearly identical to the 1040 tax form. The idea was brilliant. The form looked great. I did the same promotion and marketing that I had done for several other fun runs and was expecting about 200 people to register.

To my surprise, enrollment was so low that I ended up canceling the event. What I thought was a great idea others thought foolish. Perhaps I should have asked others for their take on the date and idea. For one thing, people finish their taxes at the last minute and are in no mood for fun. The course was a public area, the permit was inexpensive, and the marketing material was reasonable. Fortunately I was only out a small amount of money.

Vicki M., Special Events
Portland, Oregon

Money Saving Tips

- Pick dates in the slow season. Generally January and February are slower months except for Florida, Hawaii, or Southern California. Booking the event when the facility needs business is a great opener for negotiating deals.

- Booking around holidays such as Easter, Memorial Day, and Labor Day might be to your advantage.

- Pick days of the week that are slower such as Sundays. A multi-day conference arriving on Sunday and departing on Wednesday could give you substantial savings.

- For one-day meetings, Monday and Friday are slower and you can possibly get lower rates.

- If you can be flexible with dates and days of the week, ask the hotel for dates with the best rates.

- Do not be afraid to ask for better rates, especially if you are planning the event next week or next month. Facilities want to fill their rooms.

- Use the same facility for numerous events. They are likely to give you a better rate if you are a regular client.

- Consider dates when the venue has a high vacancy rate; you may be able to negotiate better rates and other benefits.

- Airfare is lower with a Saturday night stay.

- Negotiate some freebies such as complimentary suites, free parking, health club passes, or airport transportation.

- Room rental fee can be waived if room nights are picked up.

- Complimentary rooms – The usual ratio is 1:50 but ask for more. Make sure it is done on a cumulative basis not a daily basis.

CHOOSING A DESTINATION

Location, location, location! Remember you are choosing a location that will give your participants the best experience possible. Choose an environment that reinforces your goals and objectives. Your defined vision will set the tone for your location and site selection.

It is time to choose the right place for your event. Match your site to your event and audience. Make travel easy for your participants. If most of your potential participants are concentrated in one part of the country, hold your meeting in that area, preferably at an easy access gateway, making it easy for attendees to get there.

For participants who will be traveling:

- Where are they coming from?

- How convenient is it for them to travel to this location?

- Does their budget allow for travel to Hawaii?

- How is the weather at this destination during the time of year you have chosen?

- Are there are enough hotels to accommodate the participants?

- Are there enough incoming flights from around the country?

- Is it a desirable destination?

- Are there other attractions around the city?

- Can the participants afford this city?

For participants who are local:

- Is it in a convenient location?

- Is there plenty of parking?

- Is the meeting space appropriate?

The destination can be critical. Do you want to have an event in February in Buffalo, New York, or would you attract more participants to Daytona Beach, Florida? Can you imagine choosing Bozeman, Montana, for a conference site for 25,000 attendees? There would not be enough hotel rooms, a conference center large enough, or enough incoming flights. You get the picture.

CHOOSING A SITE

When you know the destination, the next task is to select the exact site. In the chapter, *The Anatomy of An Event*, we listed the vast selection of location-sites to consider when choosing the venue that best suits your defined vision. You may think you want a hotel because you are accustomed to the venue, but the destination you have chosen may have a fabulous university campus that is conveniently located with all the necessary amenities.

Site selection has never been easier. You are only a simple a mouse click away from finding Web sites with free global databases containing 40,000-plus meeting and event facilities. These sites are regularly updated with fresh information; they contain extensive photos, meeting room layouts, and contacts.

This is your opportunity to think outside the box and find a unique event space for your unique event. For assistance in finding out what is available in that city, contact the convention and visitors bureau (CVB). They are a valuable resource and will provide information concerning every aspect of the city. They are helpful because their job is to attract business. Not only will they give you a list of all the hotels and facilities in the area but will help you locate products and services that you may need for your event. Most CVBs have Web sites where you can request a meeting planners' package.

Cities actively solicit large groups to come to their area because there is so much money in large conventions, conferences, and special events. Just think of what cities go through to be in the bidding process for the Olympics.

When your destination city does not have a CVB, try the Chamber of Commerce or other planners in the area. Ask local hotels for references and names of planners who have produced in their venue.

Choose Your Sites Carefully

We had been doing our trainings in California at the same site for about four years when we got our first request to produce our week-long training in Illinois. The group that funded the event chose a university near Evanston as the site. Evanston is a wealthy area, and so we went along with the choice thinking it must be a very nice facility. We arrived on the campus very late at night and until that moment, did not know we were being housed in the freshman dorms. Everyone was housed together, staff, presenters, and all of the 100 participants. What a nightmare! What I remember are the creaky metal beds, thin tiny towels, no hangers in the closets and very dusty floors. It was almost like a prison – for one week. The participants were not very happy about the accommodations, thinking that we, the staff and faculty, were probably in some nice hotel with room service. When they found out that we were in the same facility, they didn't feel so bad and we all bonded over the experience in a wonderful way. Fortunately the cafeteria and meeting rooms turned out to be much nicer.

Moral of this story: be involved with site selection! After that experience we became involved in selecting every out-of-state training site. We negotiated with the funders not to sign any contract with any site until we were able to review it or were able to call and confirm that the venue was appropriate for all of our needs and requirements. Even when we did not get the perfect site and all of our needs were not met, we at least were aware of the situation ahead of time and could alert all parties coming to the event.

Karla Nygaard, Conference Coordinator
Sausalito, CA

Even though the story above had less than perfect accommodations, universities are a popular destination. They offer a unique atmosphere, affordability and services in combination with the advanced technological capabilities needed for the planning and management of events today. They typically offer flexible meeting and event space managed by a team of professionals.

Using Convention and Visitors Bureaus

Convention and visitor bureaus are available in most large cities to provide resources and services. They are non-profit organizations specifically formed to represent that destination. Their service will save you time by assisting you to streamline selecting the perfect site. It can be a one stop shop! They can serve as a broker or an official point of contact for event and meeting planners.

There are many advantages of using a CVB to assist in planning your event. They are a great resource even if your event is in your local area. They can create collateral material, assist with on-site logistics and registration, provide housing bureau services, develop pre- and post-conference activities such as spouse tours and special events, and help with site inspections and familiarization tours. They can provide speakers and local educational opportunities, help secure special venues, and coordinate local transportation.

CVBs give meeting planners access to a range of services, packages, and value-added extras. They can also link planners with the suppliers, from motor coach companies and caterers to off-site entertainment venues, and help meet the prerequisites of any event. Typically they can help you with events with up to 50,000 participants. Some of the larger bureaus in major cities have staff members dedicated to small events.

Many CVBs will market the destination to attendees with their promotional material, saving you money and encouraging attendance. They will also act as a liaison with community officials, thus clearing the way for special permits, street closures, and city requirements. They generate special letters of welcome from high-ranking government officials, and in some cases assist in bringing local officials to welcome your participants or well-known entertainers to entertain at your event.

Request For Proposal (RFP)

After you have a list of possible sites, write a request for proposal (RFP) to tell the potential site of your needs and request a bid based on your requirements. Include as many aspects of your event that you know, such as the following components:

RFP INFORMATION	
• Name of meeting	• Food and beverage needs
• Dates and times. (Add alternate dates if you are flexible.)	• A-V requirements
• Date you need a response by	• Participant profile (who they are, where they are coming from)
• Your goals and objectives	• Number of participants
• Your agenda	• History
• Sleeping room needs – how many and what type (singles, doubles, suites)	• Special functions planned on or off the property
• Meeting room needs – how many and what size (See agenda)	• Special dietary needs
• Rates – maximum	• Exhibit space needs
• Specific amenities needed– spa, pool, business center, food services, room service	• Support services needed (ADA compliant)
	• Non-room space available

Other questions about the facility you should ask:

FOR BUSINESS /CORPORATE – INSIDE FACILITY

- What is the room tax?
- Are there other groups booked in the hotel on those dates?
- Do you have transportation to/from the airport? What is the cost? How long does it take?
- Do you have a business center? What are the hours?
- Ask for a set of menus and audio-visual cost sheets.
- Do you have an in-house audio-visual department? If not, do you work closely with someone who does? Is there a cost for bringing in an outside company?
- Is the site close to other attractions?
- What is the weather like during our proposed dates?
- Is there plenty of parking? Do you have self-park or valet only? What are the fees?
- Does the facility have a food and beverage department?
- Do you have room service? What are the hours?
- Do you have a health club? What is the cost; what are the hours?
- Does the facility comply with the ADA (American Disabilities Act)?
- How many sleeping rooms are needed for complimentary rooms?

> ### FOR SOCIAL OR SPECIAL – OUTSIDE FACILITY/AREA
> - What other events are happening in the area on those dates?
> - Is the site close to other attractions?
> - What is the weather like during our proposed dates?
> - What kind of parking in the neighborhood? Specific parking for this venue?
> - What types of permits are necessary?
> - Will concessions and staging be needed?
> - Will we need streets to be closed?
> - How secure is the site?
> - Is there plenty of parking?
> - Is this site accessible by public transportation?

In the RFP ask for as many amenities as possible. Here is a short list of services you might request: airport transfers, early check-in times, late check-out times, complimentary coffee and tea in the rooms, complimentary meeting space, extra storage space, no receiving charges, continental breakfast in the meeting rooms, extended-stay rates, free local calls, free office space, free or reduced parking for VIPs and staff, health club access, late cutoff dates, reduced room rates for staff and speakers, upgrades for VIPs and staff, welcome gifts and notes, electrical fee reduction, discounted exhibit space, just to name a few. Do not be afraid to ask. All they can do is say yes or no.

THE SITE INSPECTION

Do a physical site inspection when possible. Absolutely do the inspection when it is local. When you travel to another city or state for the inspections, try to visit several sites during one trip. Brochures and Web sites usually enhance or show only the best side of a site. Site inspections allow you to confirm the information provided about a property and also allow you to evaluate it personally and meet the personnel. See for yourself whether the site meets your criteria. Remember, a hotel will usually give you a complimentary night or two during your stay if the site is out of your town. They should offer. If not, ask!

Do a visual walkthrough of your event before you do your site inspection to determine space requirements. You might need a 20-foot ceiling for staging and audio-visual equipment. Will you need dressing rooms for entertainers, office space for your staff, an exhibit area? Will you need loading docks, large parking areas, portable rest rooms, cooking facilities? What equipment will you need to have delivered?

Pre-arrange a meeting with the hotel department heads: the general manager, sales manager, catering manager, and the technical manager. Also take the opportunity to meet the front desk staff, banquet servers, bell captains, and concierge — the people who will directly interact with your participants. Watch the staff in their daily operations. Do they have the qualities you want? Are they accommodating, calm, helpful, friendly, professional, and prompt? Do they a deliver a consistently high level of service?

Evaluate every aspect of the hotel or venue, the sleeping rooms, meeting rooms, lobby, restaurants, recreational areas, parking, and accessibility to all parts of the hotel that your guests will be using. Observe areas that will directly affect the production end of the event. Do a walkthrough and inspect the loading docks, receiving departments, A-V and banquet equipment, dimension restrictions for delivery vehicles, loading/ unloading equipment, or electrical/lighting options. Take note whether the site has restrictions or zoning regulations or noise restrictions?

Evaluate the exact condition of the venue, cleanliness, décor, quality of the exterior of the building, as well as the interiors including the furniture, paint, and carpets. Ask whether any construction or restoration will be taking place during the dates of your event.

Walk around the neighborhood. Check the distance and ease of transfer from airports and freeways. Is there accessibility to other area attractions? Eat in their restaurants, evaluate the quality and variety of the food, confirm that the banquet food is the same quality, see other banquet displays, and witness the level of service in serving staff. Take copious notes while you do your site inspection. They will come in very handy if you visit several sites in one or two days. Or use a video camera to tape your site inspections so that you remember the property.

Know Your Neighbors

At a beautiful hotel and resort in San Diego we neglected to ask who else would be using the hotel during our multiple day seminars. It was a popular hotel on a bay, a stylish venue with weddings throughout the year. A large wedding was taking place during our event with hundreds of people. The ceremony was conducted directly outside one of our meeting rooms. After the wedding concluded and their reception began - guess what - they had a loud band and it was right next door to our evening meeting room. Both events were disruptive to our meetings. Be sure to check with the hotel and ask who your neighbors might be.

Karla Nygaard, Conference Coordinator
Sausalito, CA

THE ADA

The Americans with Disabilities Act (ADA) laws are strict and require organizers to take into consideration many important characteristics for every meeting and event. Work together with a facility so that you are in compliance. Even though it is the responsibility of the facility to provide accessibility, it is your responsibility to ensure they do so.

When creating marketing material, have space on your registration and hotel reservation forms where participants can indicate a need for special accommodations. It is your responsibility to make space on the registration form, and it will be the facility's responsibility to contact those who checked the box to determine specific needs for the room accommodations. It is against ADA laws to require that the person with the disability contact the organization or facility to expand upon their needs. This would require disabled attendees to do something non-disabled attendees do not have to do, which goes against the ADA laws.

A hearing-impaired guest may only require seating in the front row to read the speaker's lips as opposed to requiring expensive special equipment. Similarly, a sight-impaired attendee may not need Braille materials because it is likely they already own the equipment necessary to enable them to participate in the program. They may only need assistance getting around the meeting or permission to have a guide dog present. A specially built registration counter to accommodate those in wheelchairs is not necessary; simply making a clipboard available so that a wheelchair-bound attendee can fill out registration forms can suffice.

ADA laws require that individuals with disabilities inform the organization of special accommodations in advance. If they do not, the organization is not bound by the ADA laws to accommodate their needs, but of course that does not mean you will not go to any lengths to do so when appropriate.

Accommodating participants with disabilities does not have to be a challenge. Set up session and function rooms with wider aisles or remove seating to allow for wheelchairs. Doing so may affect the room set-up and capacities. Be sure to have adequate ramps if attendees or speakers will be on stage. Knowing the ADA facts and figures is important. Make sure all aspects of the facility are in compliance with ADA laws, including:

- public areas
- front desk
- barrier free/ adapted guest rooms
- hallways

- alarm systems
- door widths
- elevator button height (inside and out)

Type of Event: Performance
Duration: Two hours
Number of Attendees: 300
Type of Venue: Small theater with three banks of seats/two aisles
Subject of Story: Accommodating individuals with conflicting needs

I serve on the board of Culture! Disability! Talent! It is a disability arts organization. I was asked to be one of several ushers for a performance featuring four of our members. As part of event publicity, we included a standard invitation for people to request accommodations and a request of our own that attendees not wear perfume or scented products.

Immediately after we had seated a ticket holder with a guide dog in the center bank of seats, another ticket holder informed us that she was severely allergic to dogs. We had an obligation to make sure her risk of an allergic reaction was minimized, but we had an equal obligation not to deny the guide dog owner her right to her primary means of navigation.

Solution: We talked to the allergic woman for a few minutes about options and decided to declare the right bank of seats the "dog zone" and the left bank the "dog-free zone." We asked the guide dog owner to move to the right bank, which she did without complaint. As more people with dogs entered the theater, we steered them toward the right bank of seats, explaining why. We also made an announcement before the performance started so that people who wished to avoid the dogs could move to the left bank of seats. This appeared to be satisfactory to everyone, including the original person with the allergy.

Lesson: While not all issues involving two or more people with disabilities who have conflicting needs can be resolved this easily, it's always worth taking some time to find out details on what everyone needs as an accommodation and propose appropriate solutions.

Jane Berliss-Vincent, Director, Adult/Senior Services
Berkeley, CA, **www.cforat.org**

OUTDOOR SITES

Site inspections for outdoor events are extremely critical. The issues and challenges are vastly different from producing an event in a contained facility such as a hotel or convention center. Using public streets, parks, and public or private buildings can be a logistical headache even for the most experienced planners. For outdoor extravaganzas, many people and services are required, and the tasks are diverse, large, and complicated. Specialists in different areas should be brought in to make your event run smoothly. With outside events there will always be last-minute challenges. They are inevitable. Be prepared.

Timing is essential for outdoor productions. Many of these events are on public streets and you might find that the time limit can be tight. When you are closing off streets and controlling crowds, you may only have an eight-hour setup window for a huge public event with thousands in attendance. It may be that streets cannot be cleared for access until businesses close for the night. You may need to get in quick and get out fast. Some of the questions you might encounter when organizing an outside event are:

- What is the of power supply source?
- Where will we put the stage?
- What kind of permits will we need?
- What kind of insurance will we need?
- Do we need to get city police and fire departments involved?
- Will we need our own security?
- Where should we set up food concessions?
- How much time do we have for setup and takedown?
- Who owns the property?
- What is the weather for that time of year?

You can expect to be working with different services and vendors than you would be in a contained facility. Some of the purveyors you might encounter are the city, county, state, food vendors, lighting and technical professionals, security firms, sign makers, caterers and kitchen facilities, portable rest room companies, rental equipment, companies for equipment and supplies such as portable heaters or electricity, fences, bleachers, ticket booths, exhibits booths, barricades, tables and chairs, linens and tableware, tenting and staging.

Good vendor relationships are one important key to producing great festivals. If you are using a vendor or service for the first time, get bids from several suppliers. Stick with experienced vendors who have become familiar with the event's specific needs. Get recommendations whenever possible.

Managing Your Trash

When you have large outside events with thousands of people, expect to generate a mountain of trash. Here is a story about how the planners of the San Francisco's weekend-long Pride Celebration in 1999 built a model for trash control and recycling. Because of the success of the program, the City of San Francisco now uses the model for their large events.

The Pride Parade draws half a million participants to its June festivities. The event's large public venue is a one and a half mile parade route and 14-square-block celebration area. Two of the biggest logistical challenges have always been managing crowds and their trash. To help revelers stow their trash properly four on-site recycling stations were manned by pros who told participants about the benefits of recycling and pointed out what is recyclable and what is not. The recycling system involves blue, green, and black bins for different kinds of reusable waste and is incorporated throughout the site. When it comes to recycling, San Francisco is the leader.

Using a Destination Management Company

Going into a city for the first time and planning an event using unknown vendors and services can be overwhelming. Although the Internet, guides, and yellow pages are a good start, there is a new breed of companies that have come to the rescue: destination management companies (DMC).

You may need assistance with logistics. There are good resources, such as other event planners, but it is best to talk with a team of authentic local people in the industry. This is where the DMCs can be incredibly helpful. They make it easier to work with one vendor rather than dozens of different providers. Just how many catering companies will you want to talk with before finding the right one? The same goes for the A-V, technical equipment, transportation, and security companies. One point of contact is a great benefit. As a planner, you deal with hundreds of details so that using a good DMC can increase your bottom line.

This industry is new, raising the question are they worth the money and time? Furthermore, with the Internet, do you need a middleman? A DMC has valuable local knowledge so that they can provide logistical support, local hotel backgrounds, audio-visual services, transportation schedules, and catering possibilities.

A destination management company in a foreign country can be priceless. In Europe for example, a local DMC has inside information to assist with all your logistical needs.

CHOOSING SPEAKERS/ENTERTAINERS

The best sources of available speakers or entertainers are referrals from colleagues and friends. Get recommendations first. If your personal resources are not accessible, try a speakers' bureau to find and book the best possible choice for your needs depending on your budget and requirements. The Internet is a great resource, there are some suggestions in the Reference section of this book, find them in the local telephone book, or check professional organizations.

Speaker/Lecturer/Instructor

The right speaker or entertainment can make or break your event. Choose an expert when appropriate, someone who is motivational, captivating, and well-known in your business or just plain entertaining if that fits your vision. Choose someone who is reliable and recognizable or someone who has something new to offer your group. Will your group benefit from a sports celebrity, a best-selling author, a television personality, a well-known industry insider, or someone from within their own group?

In your planning sessions you would have decided the topic for speakers. Some events are even built around the speaker's availability which determines dates and location. Choosing keynote and final speakers is incredibly important to draw in your participants. Make sure your speakers are interesting, motivated, lively, funny, and knowledgeable. The speakers and instructors you select, be they professional trainers, volunteers, or senior management, determine whether they help you reach your goals. Ask about their presentation and their style of speaking. Ensure that they are a good fit for your audience. After you have chosen your speakers, provide them with information and guidance about your organization and share your expectations of their presentations.

After you have chosen the right individual for your program, generate a contract to state your expectations and confirm exactly what you are offering the person. (See a sample letter in the *Reference* section.) Be sure to include your request to view their presentation in advance of the event. You might need to incorporate the material into your marketing material.

Speakers may wish to use PowerPoint presentations to assist in communicating their messages. They are recommended because audiences tend to retain a greater amount of visual information.

Entertainers

For entertainment, match the music and the talent to the theme of your party and your participants. A cello quartet at a 10-year high school class reunion might be inappropriate but well suited to your parents' 50th wedding anniversary.

Certain events will require adding entertainment — even celebrities. You can locate entertainers by word-of-mouth, on the Internet, in the yellow pages, or from a recommendation from another meeting professional. Check your budget first, because speakers, entertainers, and celebrities cost money. It is common to have multiple entertainers at one event, such as a pianist for cocktail hours, a band for dancing after dinner, or several entertainers in various rooms simultaneously.

The Speakers' Budget

Speaker fees are subjective. You should always make an offer. A speaker can charge $5,000 and easily be worth much more or you might pay $15,000 and be greatly disappointed. How realistic is it to think you can get that $25,000 speaker to do a date for less? It is possible. Here are some effective strategies you can try.

Ask the speaker to give the initial speech and perhaps participate on a panel in another session, or attend the reception to greet the guests, or sit at a round table discussion. After you have them in your corner, ask them to participate in other ways that are not too imposing. You would be surprised at those who are willing to do more. Do not forget to ask them to play a round of golf with some of the high level members of your sales team or executives. They can always say no, but then, think of the excitement when they say yes!

If you have multiple meetings in multiple cities and one speaker is relevant to all events, try booking the person for a series of meetings. Given the opportunity to relay the same message to multiple audiences, the speaker may reduce his or her fee.

The Learning Annex has thousands of trainers, teachers, and best-selling authors available on a daily basis around the country. Why not tap into one of their programs? Instead of having the speaker or expert come to your event, take your participants to them. Some of their exceptional seminars bring several popular speakers together and can be purchased for as little as $49 per participant for an all-day event. Take advantage of these pre-arranged, fairly-priced opportunities and get much more for your dollar. (And leave the planning to them!)

SIGNING A CONTRACT

Your speaker or entertainer should sign a contract, either his own document or one that you provide. There is a sample contract in the Appendix.

A professional will typically request more amenities as part of performing at your event, such as first class airfare for herself and her assistants, a suite at a hotel, limos to and from the airport, specific foods, flowers, special drinks, and travel pay to and from the site.

Money Saving Tips

- Choose speakers who can also be workshop leaders.

- Find someone local to save on travel expenses.

- Negotiate the speakers' fees. Offer a flat amount rather than a fee and all expenses.

- Offer the speaking session as a chance for the speaker to update tapes/DVDs/videos. These expenses paid by the speaker could run into the thousands.

- To save on speaker expenses, consider using industry experts whose companies often pay expenses. Alternatively, use local speakers where appropriate to save on travel expenses. However, check how good they are before hiring them. You may end up with a dud!

- If dates are flexible, plan meetings around the speaker's schedule and piggyback the trip with other speaking engagements.

- If speakers have books or products to sell, consider buying them for the participants in lieu of speakers' fees.

- Pay with in-kind contributions instead of cash. For example, allow them the opportunity to sell their products, or offer them exposure to their market.

CREATING YOUR AGENDA

Every event has a beginning, middle, and an end. Each step of the way needs to be defined clearly. An agenda is the schedule for the day's activities laid out in time increments. It is your tool for getting the right information to the right people. The agenda will tell them where to be, what to expect when they get there, what to do, at what time, for how long.

There are two types of agendas. One is for the participants coming to a business or educational meeting. It is a road map for the day's schedule informing them where to go, what will be taking place, how long it will last and when to take breaks, meet for meals, or have free time.

The other is for volunteers, staff, vendors, planners, and those working behind the scenes. This agenda is for any event. It is a timeline schedule with the duties, tasks, times, and responsibilities for specific assistants or volunteers. It might say caterer arrives at 10 a.m. for beginning preparation. Florist will arrive at 10:30 a.m. with 50 bouquets of table top rounds. Tables and chairs arrive at 10:45 a.m., and the delivery of champagne is due at 11 a.m. Valerie will be on hand to sign for all the above deliveries.

Business and Educational Agendas

Create your agenda to support your defined vision. The better you are acquainted with your attendees, the more thorough your agenda will be and the more satisfied they will be. Consider the reason they are meeting and what you are going to give them, and then give them what they came for. Do this by choosing the right speakers or entertainers, or covering the appropriate topics, and give them plenty of time to absorb the information. Make sure there are breaks and time for networking and bring them together for meals or other social events.

If they came to learn about a new product, introduce the product. If they came for fun, make sure your agenda includes fun. If they came to conduct business, incorporate meetings into your agenda. If they came to be educated, teach them. Your agenda should cover all the promised topics in a timely fashion that works for the greater good.

Do a mock up of the entire agenda. Make sure to include adequate time for registration, meals, breaks, speakers, awards, and socializing. Do a visual run-through of the event and make notes of how you see it happening. Run this by your team and confirm that it works.

Be prepared for last-minute agenda changes. They may be significant requiring you to transform the event to meet a different purpose. Even a small unexpected occurrence can jolt you into an immediate change in plans. The following experience shows how the event producers quickly made the appropriate modifications to fit in the allotted time schedule.

Type of Event: Corporate Meeting/Event

Duration: Half-Day session w/working lunch – presentations; group exercises/brainstorming sessions over lunch

Number of Attendees: 350 people

Type of Venue: Hotel conference center (large gathering rooms and smaller meeting rooms)

Subject of Story: Late change in plans.

I was working with a senior technology manager and her team on plans for a department-wide planning session. We had two main goals:

1) Provide an interesting, informative series of presentations for the technology staff on business vision and technology plans for the future.

2) Provide a venue where participants could break into smaller groups to tackle ideas, questions, and issues in small brainstorming sessions, and then come together to share the results.

A week before the session, the company announced plans for Take Your Child to Work Day. The day of the planning session was identified as a primary day for children to accompany their parents to work.

Problem: The event was the antithesis of a child-oriented day. It would be boring for the children, and it was likely that the children would distract the adults, yet explicitly excluding children would send the wrong message.

Solution: We needed to embrace the concept of accommodating children as though it were another requirement of the project. I knew that the best alternative would be one that removed them from the proceedings to everyone's advantage.

I proposed an off-site planning session for children. They would spend the first 30 minutes with the adults during the welcome session. Then they would be escorted out to their own creative, fun-filled day! An advance invitation to adult participants, with another invitation specifically for children, would ensure that everyone was clear on the day's program.

The proposal was accepted. I would be working with the adults; I needed someone to work with the children. On very short notice, I called two associates (one of them Shannon!) and asked, begged, pleaded, implored, and beseeched them for help!

About 40 children accompanied their parents to the event. They attended the welcome session and were then escorted out to their own off-site meeting. There they worked in teams to brainstorm how we would all use technology in the future for monetary transactions. Each team designed and developed a presentation. Then, the children returned to the adult session where each team delivered their presentation.

The event was a win-win for everyone. The children were beaming as they accepted their recognition certificates. We were rated excellent in the feedback.

Lesson learned:

- Some opportunities masquerade as problems.

- Contain a problem, but also try to see how it can work to your advantage.

- Children are extraordinarily imaginative. (I'm convinced some of them have gone on to be engineers!)

Susan Mason
Mason and Wall Communications

Money Saving Tips

- Evaluate the number of breakout sessions. By reducing them you can save food and beverage costs, speakers' fees, audio-visual costs, and room rental fees.

- Book all speakers' presentations for the same room if they have the same audio-visual needs.

Social and Special Events Agendas

Timing for social and special events is very critical. Set-up can be time-consuming. Consider stages, lighting, tenting, tables, chairs, booths, and signs, electricity, barricades, and other specific equipment. It can be demanding because there is often a short time to get the stage set. Dozens of vendors, volunteers, and staff may arrive about the same time and will be coming and going frequently. It is imperative that someone is in charge of verifying the arrival of these people, giving the correct directions to them and confirming that they are equipped to do their jobs.

The agenda for these events may be down to the minute, listing who is in charge, exactly what is happening, where it is happening, and who is coming or going. There could be several schedules for an event that may last only two hours. You will have a list for catering people, transportation company, registration team, decorators, and designers; the head coordinator will be in charge of all the staff leaders working each area. There may be hundreds of volunteers requiring several leaders to assign and direct suppliers and vendors.

Hundreds of things can be going on simultaneously and the more that is written down and confirmed, the better off everyone will be. You will know exactly when the bakery truck is arriving, the exact quantities they are to deliver, and who will meet them and sign for the delivery. As you can see, these agendas are powerful. They can save the day if one key person is absent so that you can hand off the schedule to someone else to pick up and run that responsibility.

Creating the Atmosphere

reating an atmosphere that will keep your participants comfortable, well cared for, secure, and satisfied should be among your top priorities. Customer satisfaction is elevated when the participants are getting what they came for and more. If they came to meet the new board members or sponsors, introduce them and have them mingle with the participants. If they came to learn new techniques, teach them! If they came to have fun, give it to them! Make them comfortable while they are there. When you do this, your participants will walk away from your event fulfilled. When the customer is satisfied you have a successful event!

Customer satisfaction means setting up the venue so that maneuvering is easy, presenting the best audio-visual arrangement for all the participants, having easy access to registrations, tickets, materials, and enough food and beverages for fulfillment. You will need to make the surroundings comfortable and conducive to the ongoing activities; you will need to feed participants and equip them with all the materials needed to fulfill their reasons for coming. The result is that you will be guaranteed a good reputation and valuable word of mouth publicity.

Technology plays a large role in creating your atmosphere. Using the newest equipment is so important that we have an entire chapter in this guide called *Staying on Top of Technology*. Look there for the most up-to-date electronic and audio-visual equipment, and computer and Internet paraphernalia. In this chapter we look at the reasons your event may require equipment, something that will help determine the venue. Many venues have not moved up to the 21st Century and are not capable of doing so even with help from outside companies.

ROOM SET-UP

Turning a typical meeting space into a learning environment is more than arranging chairs and tables in classroom style. Room set up, lighting, sound, temperature, supplies, and amenities are critical to successful learning.

Room set-up can mean the difference between success and failure. If the participants are uncomfortable, they will remember that above all else. Make sure the room is set up to be beneficial to the event you are producing.

People learn more when they interact with other people. A session that allows for networking among peers is often more valuable than just one or two speakers talking to an audience all day. A room that allows for movement and networking is important. You should face your audience toward the long wall in any room to expose more people to the front/stage area, especially important if you have a long, narrow room. Consider the direction people are entering the room. Have them enter from the back. Do not have people entering from the front while the speaker is talking or you will have constant interruptions and embarrassed late-comers.

Try to visit the meeting room before deciding on a room setup so that you have first-hand knowledge of how the room will work for you, the participants, and the speakers. Find out if there is another meeting scheduled in the room before yours is to begin. Know what time they will finish so that you have enough time to check the room before your meeting begins. Also find out if there are other meetings going on next to your room and make sure that the walls will filter out their noise.

The typical room layouts seen in the diagrams below are still commonly used and work well when you take into consideration the objectives of the event. Look at the following overviews to determine the best layout design for your function.

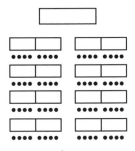

Classroom Style: This layout is best suited when participants will be taking notes, using a computer, or referring to material of some kind. This is not a great setup when you want a lot of networking. It is typically used for a longer session and when the presenter will be doing most of the talking.

Hollow Square or Rectangle Style: This setup is nice for educational sessions, large committee meetings, boards of directors, or staff meetings.

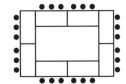

Theatre Style: Best use here is when maximum seating capacity is needed. This design is used when speakers are on stage and or they will be showing presentations. Not practical when attendees must take notes.

Banquet Style: This style is typically used for meal functions. It is also good for small breakouts or committees where networking and note-taking are required.

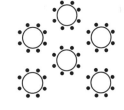

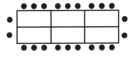

Conference Style: Used for board or committee meetings where interaction will be anticipated. This can also be good for food and beverage functions for small gatherings.

U-shape Style: Good for board and committee meetings and break-out session. Good for meetings that involve A-V presentations. This is style can serve for banquets as well.

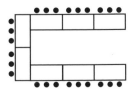

Always work with the banquet department of the venue because they will know the best arrangement for each of their rooms. You will need to be specific in your instructions and needs.

During a meeting a speaker was at the podium on stage. To the side of the podium were a table and chairs. Being a motivational speaker, he moved around as he spoke and would rest his hands on the chair. Each time the chair moved ever so slightly until one leg slipped off the stage unnoticed. The next time he rested his hands on it, the chair tumbled off the stage and he followed. Fortunately he was not hurt. He popped up quickly and was back on stage in a flash continuing his presentation.

Anonymous

Money Saving Tips

- Wherever possible, use theater style (where only chairs are used). It is less labor-intensive than classroom-style (which includes both table and chairs), thus lowering setup costs. Also, plan to keep set-ups the same from day to day.

- Cut down on classroom-style set-ups for some of the rooms. They require more labor, more space, and are slower to turn into another setting compared to theater style.

- Work with groups in the hotel before and after your event. Try sharing room set-up and maybe even speakers and audio-visual equipment.

- Use the same room with two setups. For example, use the room classroom-style for the course and banquet-style for lunch and breaks. Put up screens or use plants to divide the space.

REGISTRATION AREA SET-UP/TICKET SALES

Your participants' first encounter with the event will be the registration tables. Make sure this area runs smoothly: if it does not, you appear disorganized and unprepared. Work with the venue to come up with the best scenario possible for the number of people you are expecting.

The layout of your registration area is a vital consideration. It will be a focal point. When laying out this area, pretend you are an attendee and walk through the process. Make it easy and quick and avoid long lines whenever possible. If they have to complete the registration on-site, make it easy to complete the form. You might want to use computer kiosks with online registration. When setting up the layout consider the following points:

- Is the registration area located in a central place?

- Which direction will people enter from?

- Can they see the signs?

- Is there enough room for lines of people?

- Can people with disabilities easily register?

- Is there a place attendees can go if they have questions or need time to fill out forms?

- Can attendees pick up their materials from any of the registration staff or must they go to another table or booth?

- Do you need a special registration area for exhibitors, VIPs, speakers, or sponsors?

- Will you have on-site registration for those who did not register early?

- Do you need to collect payment?

- Do you need a phone line for credit card verification?

- Do you need Internet access?

- Do you need tables for displays, pamphlets, or handouts?

- Do you need tables for vendors? Hotel staff?

AUDIO-VISUAL REQUIREMENTS

Most events will require some audio-visual equipment. There is an entire chapter in this book devoted to technology with emphasis on A-V needs of events of all kinds. See the chapter on *Staying on Top of Technology*. The day of the slide projector and microphone is gone. Today the industry is so technically sophisticated, you may require training.

Make sure to order only what you require because audio-visual equipment is not cheap, but if done well, it will enhance your meeting. Done poorly, it is a distraction for your participants and you, the coordinator, because you have to deal with it, usually at the last minute. Make sure your participants can see and hear the speakers and entertainment and are able to participate fully in the event.

The technological progression has taken us from the microphone and the overhead projector to the slide projector, to computer aided PowerPoint presentations to Web casting and T1 lines for multiple computer access.

Today's speakers, entertainers, and even participants expect the latest technology: computerized presentations, wide screens for extra large rooms or simulcast into additional rooms, Internet access, satellite downlinks, and video conferencing. Confirm with your speakers and entertainers just exactly what their needs are for their presentations.

Discuss with your venue and the audio-visual company what your needs will be and confirm that they are in the position to meet your standards. Ask them for testimonials or discuss what sets them apart from other companies. Ask if they have any specialized services such as state of the art technology in lighting, sound, staging, or rigging. Make sure you budget for all of it.

Whether you use your venue's service or an outside company, make sure they are equipped to handle any unexpected changes such as replacement equipment or last-minute additions. Do they have extra equipment on-site or are they connected to an outside company that will respond immediately to your needs? Find out how long the staff has been with the facility and know how familiar they are with the staff and the facility itself. Make sure they are involved in all of the pre-event meetings so that they are current with any and all changes.

Make certain that the A-V company you hire is properly insured. The contract should include the insurance requirements. In particular, the company should carry at least $2 million in liability insurance coverage and workers' compensation insurance. Ask them to provide you with proof (a certificate) of their liability insurance coverage. Depending on your event and whether you have your own insurance, you may request that you and your client are listed as insured on their policy, providing you with extra insurance coverage.

ON-SITE INTERNET ACCESS

Your technology-savvy participants will expect high speed Internet access while they are attending your function, especially if it keeps them away from the office for more than a day. We all are conditioned to "stay in touch" with our work, our families, and our daily Internet habits. The biggest problem for you, the planner, or the organization is budget. Can you afford it?

The use of kiosks at outdoor events is just as common as finding public computers in hotels and convention centers. At a high profile triathlon in San Francisco and there were at least 15 stand-alone computers for participants, spectators, anyone passing by to add comments, give feedback, take surveys, and print coupons. They were paid for by the sponsor of the event but within the applications on the computer, other exhibitors had the opportunity to advertise their products as well.

Take these few ideas into consideration when figuring out Internet providers and their services at the venue. Have a good idea what the high speed access will be used for since all applications are not the same. If participants simply want to check their e-mail throughout the conference, one system can be used. However, if you have many uses such as video conferencing, Web streaming, instant messaging, a different system will be needed altogether. Especially find out what your speakers and workshop leaders will need and tie that in with what the participants expect.

Check with the venue to see what type of Internet security system they have. They may have a firewall that would inhibit the use of many types of communications. At the same time find out what type of service the venue currently has, who is their provider, and what kind of technical support they have on-site or on contract? How fast can they respond to technical difficulties? Is an on-site technician required?

Some service providers will simply install the system without support while others give ongoing support to the contract's end. Take advantage of the venue's technical support contract if there is one. Sometimes the venue will have technical support on staff. Whatever the case may be, know what is offered before signing a contract or choosing that particular venue.

You can profit by having computers with Internet access for your attendees. Your own homepage can be used as an advertising tool, a message service, and an opportunity for others to advertise. Know the limits and potential problems such as configuration changes on the computers, or unintentional infection from viruses. Be mindful of how you set up access for your participants. Do not just plug in several computers with access. Have professionals create a shell that will protect the system and limit access to what the guests might need. They can also create time limits, redirect to your homepage, or post messages regularly relating to the event.

Budgeting your Internet access

Compare pricing when planning this amenity. If the venue has a provider, you probably will have to use them. If not, get bids from several businesses. Prices will vary for the different services you will want or need. You can be charged for different types of connections and for the number of computers you will use. Plan on paying for the original connection, a fee per computer, and a fee per computer connection.

Should you charge for the connection?

Attendees will most likely expect it to be free, but here is your opportunity to use sponsorship dollars. You might be able to offset some of the expense by charging a few more dollars in the registration fee. If you choose to have the computers at no cost to your attendees, put that information in your marketing material. People are pleased if they do not have to carry their computers when they travel. You can make it a win-win-win situation: give the participants what they want, offer a great opportunity for a sponsor, and you look great by providing this terrific resource.

Here is an audio-visual plan.

- If you are in the early stages of identifying your audio-visual needs, prepare a request for proposal with your requirements and get at least two bids. Get the bids even if you know you will use the in-house company to give yourself an idea of costs that you can use as leverage with the in-house company. Make sure you know the cost of equipment, labor, service fees, and how taxes are calculated.

- Consider signing a contract early with the audio-visual company to lock in rates.

- Several weeks before your meeting (before you order any audio-visual equipment) get the name of the in-house audio-visual manager and call to introduce yourself. Find out the name and contact information of the individual you will be working with on-site and make sure all of your audio-visual requirements go through that person.

- Provide a diagram. Get a floor plan of your meeting room directly from the hotel. Sketch in your preferences for setting up the room. Then work with the audio-visual staff.

- Let the audio-visual company know your budget and ask them to work with you. When they know your goals and your budget, they will be better equipped to fulfill your needs.

Be sure to have good technical support on-site the days of the event! There is nothing more frustrating than a VCR, computer, or sound system that breaks down at a crucial moment. Be sure to check all equipment before the event starts. Some venues will charge extra for this service, but it is well worth the money.

Money Saving Tips

- Look outside the hotel for possible audio-visual suppliers whose prices may be more competitive than those in-house. However, the hotel may match the other supplier's prices if asked.

- If you have both general session and breakout rooms, try to use the general session room as one of your breakouts to save on audio-visual costs.

- When on-site, consider purchasing laser pointers, flip charts, and easels. Many times a single day's cost of renting these items equals the purchase price! Plus, buy spares and you can give the laser pointers away as gifts for the speakers.

- Limit the number of microphones needed. Check whether the hotel supplies a complimentary microphone in each meeting room. Skirt a cocktail table instead of renting special carts for A-V equipment.

- Limit use of wireless microphones.

- Use one microphone for two speakers.

- Re-confirm speakers' audio-visual needs. Avoid ordering more equipment than necessary.

- Bring your own equipment.

MATERIAL AND PROMOTIONAL GIFTS

We all enjoy receiving a gift. It is natural and we just like it! Event materials and mementos come in all different shapes and sizes. There are conference packets, name tags, programs, handouts, ribbons, giveaways (coffee mugs, T-shirts with logos), certificates, and often a tote bag to carry them all in. Leaving with more stuff than you came with has become a tradition when attending conferences, trade shows, and conventions. Promotional items for a sports event will differ greatly from what is given at a corporate team-building seminar. Whatever it is, it must be in line with the vision. But keep in mind your environmental standards. A gift may not be appropriate unless it is within the guidelines and meets your standards.

The choice of your gift will be a part of your goals and objectives and will depend on your budget. It is a great form of publicity and marketing that can keep on working well after your event is over.

At a conference, name tags are a must but not necessary at the town's May Day parade or a wedding. However, a program of the parade would be nice and T-shirts with the logo and dates could be relevant. A special keepsake for a wedding is traditional showing the name of the bride and groom and their wedding date. You are only limited by your imagination and budget as to what you can offer your attendees. If something has worked in the past, keep the item but jazz it up a bit or change it slightly and give it a new twist.

- Know the defined vision.

- What has been used in the past?

- What worked and what did not?

- Does it fit within the environmental standards guidelines?

Are these gifts important or appropriate?

It depends on the event itself. If the gift is a reminder of an enjoyable event and your gracious hospitality, your logo is emblazed on the item, and it will be used and seen for years to come that is a great marketing device! A little extra effort, creativity, and expense can go a long way in getting the attention of the participants and making them feel special.

Decide whether the promotional items should be useful or memorable before you choose them. They must be suitable, useful, thoughtful, imaginative, relevant, and increase name recognition. Do not just pick something to have something. Make it work for you! Are you carrying a canvas bag or using a pen, a money clip, a paper weight on your desk that has a company logo from an event you attended?

Do not give them a throwaway souvenir. Stick to something they will really love, like an iTunes gift certificate or organic, fair-trade chocolates, or think of something unique such as planting trees in their names at your local park or calculate the amount of money to donate to one of the zero emission companies to offset travel.

Food and
Beverage

*P*lanning for food and beverage at your events can be complicated and time-consuming, but the good news is that most hotels, caterers, and restaurants will work closely with you to plan the perfect menu choices. They have great suggestions and will help you create menus especially for your needs. They will know what is in season and what would be best served on your particular dates, and since they are experts they can easily work within your budget. Ultimately, it is your job to research all of your options.

Knowledge of your audience is important when choosing menu items. People are more health conscience today about foods. It is critical to offer participants food and drinks that will enhance their ability to learn and pay attention versus something that might spike energy levels or induce drowsiness. What is the difference between a "pick-me-up" and a "space-me-out" afternoon snack?

Food will be one of your biggest expenses whether you are sitting down to a full-course dinner, serving coffee and snacks for a couple days of morning and afternoon breaks, hiring outside vendors to set up shop at your event, or having a cocktail reception. Know how much you can spend and create your menus accordingly. We offer many cost-cutting suggestions that will provide your participants with quality of food and beverages.

The liabilities of serving alcohol are of great concern today. The only way to eliminate liquor liability is to eliminate alcohol from your event, but if that is not an option, you can take steps to keep your attendees from overindulging, decreasing your liability risks.

KNOW YOUR AUDIENCE

Take into consideration the age, nationality, gender, religion, and special meal circumstances of your participants. Some may require low carbohydrate or low sodium meals, high protein, low fat, no sugar, kosher, or vegetarian dishes. Some may have food allergies. Make sure you put these choices in your registration forms.

There will always be the group that loves their meat and potatoes, but there are those more influential groups who want sashimi tuna pierced on forks displayed handles down, or a quick grab shrimp hanging from tree branches, stuffed lobster tail, or a buffet station where wait staff is dressed in themed costumes serving tastes of warm liquid Belgian chocolate over some decadent imported vanilla cookies. That is why knowing your audience is key to ordering the appropriate meal. The meal that would be inappropriate for the National Cattlemen's Association could be perfect for a *Fortune* 500 CEO retirement party.

GUARANTEEING YOUR NUMBERS

As your event nears, you will be required to give the venue your estimated number of participants. You will pay for the number of meals that you set, even if they are no-shows. The final numbers are usually required 72 hours before the event. Typically a facility will prepare for 3 percent to 10 percent above the number you submit depending on the size of your group. The larger the group the fewer extra meals they will prepare.

The amount of food and money that is wasted during an event can be excessive. While donating leftover food to charitable organizations makes us feel good, ordering appropriately from the beginning and making the effort to guarantee accurately is a skill that can reduce costs significantly and is environmentally fitting.

Factors That Impact Your Numbers

Factors that impact the number of people attending meal functions, especially for a multi day event:

- Watch the number of hotel departures for each day of the meeting; those departing that day will most likely not be attending that night's dinner function.

- Watch the weather forecast; a beautiful day will encourage attendees to skip a banquet lunch function, while a rainy or cold day will cause most to attend.

- Be aware of your destination and what is around the venue. People like to sight-see when they are away and the more interesting things to do, the more people will adventure out of the meetings and meal functions.

- Pay attention to the timing of the function; if sessions end at 5 p.m. and a reception starts at 7 p.m., many attendees will not come back.

- Programming also affects guarantee management. Featuring a unique speaker, entertainment, or awards presentations during a meal function will encourage more attendees to participate.

WORKING WITH THE VENUE AND CATERER

Although the catering manager, convention services manager, food and beverage director, chef, or a hired caterer will have wonderful suggestions, keep the following tips in mind to get the best value and make sure meals, banquets, coffee breaks, and receptions are to your satisfaction.

- Consult with the chef for ideas and special requests. Create your own list of options; you do not have to order off the menu.

- Choose healthy and high-quality foods that are in season.

- For large, important meal functions, make arrangements to do a tasting. Most facilities will allow advance taste testing. Do a tasting if you are indecisive about a couple of selections.

- Know the food and beverage policies. Find out what is allowed. Most facilities will charge a fee to bring your own food and beverage, or they will simply not allow you to do so. Some organizations print their logo on prepackaged food and beverages and distribute these items to the participants. Try to negotiate this, if possible. It can amount to considerable savings.

- Find out how many servers and bartenders will be assigned to your functions. Service levels vary from facility to facility.

- Consider the appropriate type of service for a meal. Need a quick lunch? A box lunch might be the answer. Want people to mingle? Try a buffet. Service can vary according to a meeting's aims and goals. When buffets are used, make sure that the line is double and that there is at least one double-sided buffet line for every 75 to 100 people.

- Use decorative props and themes for breaks and meals. Ask the event venue about decorations in its inventory. Try to negotiate free use of these materials or rent props from event-planning companies.

- All meeting facilities have banquet menus. You will have the option of selecting plated meals, buffets, break packages, and à la carte items. They are sold either at a per-person price or by the dozen, gallon, or piece. All prices are then subject to applicable service charge or gratuity and taxes. Find out the tax and service charge or gratuity percentages and factor them into your budget. On average, they are 20 percent to 30 percent of the total food and beverage bill.

- Get menus in the beginning of the booking process and review prices and options. Ask about the catering policies and a general information sheet. These explain specific food and beverage policies and might include their deadlines for receiving your menu selections, guarantees of attendance, table linen choices, floral arrangements, ice carvings, coat checks, extra labor charges, liquor liability issues, and liability statements.

- Negotiate firm menu prices when you book a meeting at a facility. Most facilities will guarantee food and beverage prices six to nine months in advance. You can request a guarantee for current menu prices or get a date through which prices are guaranteed.

COST-CUTTING SUGGESTIONS

With food and beverage playing such an important role in most events, this section will assist you in cutting your costs while maintaining quality and satisfaction. We have to remember our vision and preserve our goals and objectives. Perhaps money is not an object for your event, but it is likely that these suggestions can reduce waste, suggest ideas for more appropriate choices, and provide tips for working with the professionals.

General Suggestions

When looking to lower the price of your lunch or dinner, request a six-ounce instead of eight-ounce chicken breast or steak. Reducing the portion size of the accompanying side dishes does not help at all. Have heaping sides of rice or pasta or potatoes or other delicious non-meat plates. Instead of serving dessert at lunch, serve cookies, brownies or something sweet at the afternoon break.

When there is another larger group in the same hotel, it is often common that the smaller group can be served the same menu as the larger group. This is called "ganging" and it is possible the facility may reduce the price of your meal if you choose this option.

Buffet meals are more expensive than plated meals. You can also choose a less expensive meal, but make it more formal by requesting a formal service style. While there may be service charges associated with more formal service, the savings on the menu price may more than make up for them.

Strategically located tables can alter the amount of food consumed whether it is a breakfast buffet, refreshment breaks, or reception stations. Place them where they are not so readily accessible for seconds or thirds. Placing more expensive items in harder to access places can reduce consumption such as placing shrimp or carving stations at the back of the room for receptions.

There is a very fine line you can cross here when trying to save costs. If food and beverage are too difficult to access, especially if there are long lines, you are likely to receive negative feedback and complaints from your participants.

Order bulk portions versus per person items, especially for continental breakfasts and refreshment breaks. While it is easier for planners to order based on the number of people attending, per person packages are more expensive because facilities must provide enough food for the number of people you have guaranteed regardless of whether the food is consumed.

Receptions and Cocktail Parties

Cocktail receptions with hors d'oeuvres and liquor can be one of the most difficult food and beverage functions to manage in terms of cutting costs without reducing quality. However, a few tips can help:

- Use butler style service for hors d'oeuvres.

- Use smaller plates on buffet tables—less will be consumed.

- Put more expensive items toward the back of the room.

- Use cheese platters and crudités; they offer a large amount of food for less price.

- Use tray service for wine and soft drinks near the entrance, with full-service bars in the back. People who start with wine out of convenience will continue.

- Shorten cocktail parties and receptions—even 15 minutes can save you money.

- Use drink tickets instead of an open bar. Give each participant two or three tickets.

- Beer and wine are less expensive than hard liquor.

- Instruct bartenders not serve doubles.

- When it comes to hors d'oeuvres, try fewer choices in larger quantities rather than a large selection in smaller quantities. Remember to avoid the shrimp. People inhale it.

- Avoid salty foods during receptions as it encourages people to drink more.

- Go for domestic rather than imported wines and beer. Use house brands rather than premium.

- Check whether the hotel has dead stock wine available

(wine that is no longer on the wine list). You may be able to negotiate a great price for some really good quality wine.

Serving Wine at Dinner

Wasting wine is very typical when precautions are not taken. With controlled conditions, having wine with dinner can be possible without breaking the bank. Take these tips into consideration:

- Open one bottle of each type of wine at a time.

- Start wine service after the salad or appetizer is served.

- Offer the wine. Do not just pour for everyone.

- Only refill wine when asked.

- Consider limiting the total number of bottles. Instruct servers to consult the planner when more is asked for.

- Have time limit for service; suspend the wine service at a specific time especially if it is late in the dinner.

Coffee Breaks and Continental Breakfasts

There are many ways to reduce spending for these meal functions. Be creative and work with the venue to assist with these recommendations:

Order "on consumption" when possible for bottled water, soda, and prepackaged food items such as granola bars, bags of chips, yogurt, whole fruit, power bars, cookies, and brownies. Or eliminate the bottled water and serve water in a pitcher.

In some facilities, one gallon of coffee can cost $90 to $100 dollars and more, and the same price may be charged for hot water. Supervision and advanced planning are needed to result in significant savings. Order only what is needed, based on the number of people, the time of day, and the demographics of the group, and put controls in place for replenishing these beverages.

A gallon of coffee or decaf or hot water provides 18 to 20 cups or 14 to 16 mugs of coffee. Depending upon the length of the event, you can figure two cups per person of coffee/decaf/tea combined. Again knowing your audience is key to your ordering suitable amounts. Younger groups tend to consume more soft drinks than coffee, which means coffee orders can be reduced.

Many facilities either automatically replenish coffee as it is consumed, or replenish at specific times to original levels. Specify exact procedures for refilling beverages, such as checking with you before replenishing; not replenishing anything in the last five to ten minutes of a continental breakfast or refreshment break; or replenishing a certain amount of coffee/decaf/hot water at a certain time.

When food is left over from the continental breakfast, have it stored and used at the mid-morning breaks and likewise for leftovers from the morning break saved and used for the afternoon break. Order items that can be purchased on a consumption basis only or order them by the dozens for afternoon breaks.

A few more cost saving tips:

- Use any leftover food, not purchased on consumption, for the next break. Items like breakfast breads can be reused and put out at the mid-morning break. Unused food can also be delivered to the staff office or donated to a local shelter or soup kitchen.

- Serve mini-Danishes, muffins and doughnuts, or cut larger servings in half. Many people (especially women and dieters) only want half to start with. Alternatively, serve a continental breakfast instead of a full breakfast buffet.

- Add yogurt or cereals to dress up a continental breakfast.

- Use packaged items at breaks and be charged for consumption only. They can be used again.

- Go for sodas rather than more expensive mineral waters.

Timelines For Meals

The following are some time frames to take into consideration when creating your agenda for meal service. Generally speaking, follow these guidelines and as always, they vary depending on your group, your finances, your venue, and your original vision. Use this as a starting point. Always defer to hotel/caterer for suggestions.

TYPE OF FUNCTION	TIME ALLOTMENT	STAFF PER PERSON	NOTES
Continental breakfast	30 minutes to 1 hour	One buffet and one server up to 120 people	
Full Breakfast	One hour	If buffet, 1 server Sit down – 1 server per 30+ guests	Only about 50 percent of participants will attend. Buffet is best.
Breaks between meetings	Minimum of 30 minutes	One server up to 100 people	Time for rest room, phone calls, networking.
Lunch	Minimum of 90 minutes	Sit down – 1 server per 30+ guests	Partial pre-set tables are helpful.

TYPE OF FUNCTION	TIME ALLOTMENT	STAFF PER PERSON	NOTES
Receptions	Variable depending on whether dinner is to follow.	One server per 50 people	Will depend how much food is served or at all and type of bar setup.
Dinner	Two hours	Sit down – 1 server per 30+ guests	If formal, increase staff – 1 per 20

ALCOHOL LIABILITY

Every planner must consider the gravity of dealing with intoxicated participants, underage drinking, and drunk driving when providing alcohol at events whether it is inside a contained facility or outdoor and open to the public. This is serious business as you could be held responsible or sued if something were to go wrong. Most liquor laws mandate that it is an offense to allow individuals to become intoxicated or to serve individuals who are already intoxicated.

When you hire a hotel or caterer to sell or serve alcohol at your event, be sure that the vendor is compliant with state and local licensing and insurance regulations. If your server organization has no insurance, you or your company may be responsible for monetary damages.

Perhaps the best way to reduce your liability is to create an environment that discourages over-consumption. For example, limit the number of bartenders, making it harder to get a drink. Hold functions earlier in the evening perhaps from 5 to 6 p.m. when people are less inclined to drink heavily, or limit receptions to one hour.

Here are some concerns and issues you should be aware of when serving alcohol at your event.

- Do not purchase and serve alcohol yourself. Let the facility or caterer provide and serve the alcohol. Doing so yourself may be a less expensive route but it increases your liability.

- Ask what the venue policies are for service and how servers have been trained.

- Follow certain steps to prevent overindulgence by placing tent cards at the bar urging attendees to exercise good judgment and drink responsibly.

- Provide transportation or designated drivers — even designated walkers, especially for those staying in the hotel but have trouble getting to their rooms without injuring themselves or abusing others verbally or physically.

- If off-site or as participants leave event, include a safe transportation plan. Encourage designated driver programs.

- Liquor liability insurance is not covered by standard provisions of general liability insurance. A rider may be necessary for your event. Note: coverage does not include situations in which alcohol service is in violation of a statute, ordinance, or regulation; a minor is served; or an already intoxicated person is served.

- Put an indemnification clause in your contract with the facility or caterer providing and serving the alcohol, making it clear that the facility or caterer will indemnify, defend, and hold harmless the company from and against all liability arising from alcohol-related incidents.

- Bartenders and servers are not to serve any individuals who appear inebriated or under the influence of alcohol. Require servers to refuse service to intoxicated guests.

- If the event is outside, use only plastic glasses and

aluminum cans to prevent glass from being used as weapons during fights.

- Permit only regular drinks — no doubles.

- Have a good selection of non-alcoholic and low-alcohol beverages available at a reduced rate or complimentary.

- Price non-alcoholic drinks at a 30 percent discount from drinks containing alcohol.

- Eliminate last call to avoid guests from stocking up before the bar closes.

Outdoor events serving or selling alcohol present different challenges, especially when the event is open to the public and in an area with no specific perimeters or fencing to contain the crowd. Balancing fun and festivities with responsible planning is imperative.

Secure your site. Alcohol related risks can present themselves even before the participant enters the event. Hire uniformed security staff to monitor the outside areas such as parking lots to prevent intoxicated participants from entering the venue or driving away.

Good monitoring of IDs is also a must. It is helpful to have clear, concise rules posted at the entrance regarding general conduct and alcohol in particular. Train your staff on the procedures and guidelines that you established for your event.

Many groups and organizers learn the hard way about alcohol problems and liability. When your event suffers from fights, injuries, or citations related to drinking, the quality of your event is jeopardized. Plan ahead and be prepared with guidelines, insurance, security, and take all the precautions possible.

$$\mathscr{Marketing}$$
$$\mathscr{Your\ Event}$$

Getting the word out and carrying your message to your potential guests is essential! Whether your participants are invited, required to attend, or willing to pay to come to your event, they need to know what your event is all about. They need to know when, where, why, how much, and what they should wear. Good marketing and promotional materials will be your vehicle to carry your message. They allow prospective participants to understand what you are offering, why they need to attend, and what is in it for them. Are you offering something significant and meaningful? You must demonstrate the benefits and value of attending your event throughout these materials. Make the information clear and understandable.

The defined vision plays an important role in your message and all of your promotional material from this point. Your goals and objectives are repackaged into a positive marketing campaign. The message you are sending must be powerful, set the tone, embrace your potential participants, and entice them to come.

From your planning sessions, you came up with some methods for "getting your message out." You may have decided it would be through advertisements, publicity, public relations, direct mail, an e-mail blast, or promotions. Use what works best for you and your event.

Knowing and reaching your target market is indispensable, but successfully getting the message to them clearly is always a challenge. Depending on the type of event, you will have all sorts of participants: some will be required to come, some will pay their own way, others will come at the expense of their companies, and some will just be invited free of charge. Regardless of their reason for coming, you must reach them with an effective and timely invitation.

When you do not have a list of your target market it is imperative that you find one or begin developing one. One way to begin this process is through networking, meaning that you hit the business meeting circuit, speak with friends and business associates, and go to trade shows.

Your invitation should create anticipation and enthusiasm for your event. It is the primary function of your message that will be reflected in every piece of material you produce. Your marketing and promotional material can come in hundreds of different styles and be delivered in as many ways. Most often it will include a registration form.

For many events, marketing is handled by an individual or group of specialists. A non-profit organization may have a public relations committee, while a corporation might have a marketing department or director on staff. Larger corporations may have a public relations firm or advertising company on retainer. Whether you are doing it yourself or working with others, begin a plan. Start early to design your promotional material. Do not miss important deadlines because your marketing copy is being edited late.

PROMOTING YOUR EVENT

Marketing and publicity material is imperative to promote your event. The material you create essentially invites someone to come to your event by providing as much information about what it offers and how to become a participant. Your invitation can be a poster, party invitation, full-color brochure, one-page flyer, radio spot, newspaper ad, or all the above. The choice is yours; just get the message out.

Simple or complicated, there are hundreds of ways to get your message out. The key is giving yourself enough time to create the material successfully and completely. There is nothing worse than sending out 5,000 flyers only to discover you put the wrong phone number in the text. Here are some promotional possibilities: e-mail blasts, fax distribution, direct mailing, networking, partnerships with other organizations, advertising, telemarketing, past participants, press releases, publicity, referral, Web site, Internet, word of mouth, blogs, and podcasts.

Weigh out the benefits of advertising dollars versus memorable amenities. Consider carefully, do you really need that four-page full-color brochure that will cost an arm and a leg or would you rather create a smaller, less expensive piece and spend the savings on something special for the participants? Making the event more exciting and memorable might be worth more than the marketing material. They will not remember the brochure as much as the trio singing in the background during lunch or the delicious croissants served every morning with freshly brewed rich coffee.

When I was doing sporting events I found that one of the best ways to get to my target market was to attend similar events and go around the parking lot and place flyers under the windshield wipers of each car. Each flyer would have a registration form as well as all the information a participant would need to know about the event. The time, place, event, cost, address, and phone number in the promotion. I would mark each form with a code to let me know where it came from. This way I could keep track of where my efforts worked the best. This was well before the invention of Web sites or the Internet. But this type of marketing effort is still good today. Remember, use recycled paper and note your Web site address. The key is to make it easy for people to participate.

Kathy T, Columbus Ohio

If the telephone is not ringing and the returned RSVP forms are not in your mailbox, you may need to do something different. But what?

The flyer itself may be perfect, but it must be in the hands of the right people. The flyer may be reaching the right people, but not doing a good enough job of motivating them to take action. The problem is with this method of marketing is that it is hard to get feedback on what specifically you need to change.

Ask yourself, have you got the right brochure reaching the wrong people, the wrong brochure reaching the right people, or worst of all, the wrong brochure reaching the wrong people! One thing for sure is that when you have the right brochure reaching the right people, you are well on your way to ensuring that your next event is a raging success.

Publicity and word of mouth are the least risky and most effective means of promotion. And they are free. Send press releases to the media or to your potential participants about your event. Be specific and grab their attention. Send this information to other business and organizations as well and let them network for you.

This guide is not going to tell you or suggest that you need advertising or tell you the type of advertising you need, but we have listed different styles of advertising options. You will know whether you need advertising from your defined vision and the type of event you are having. But most importantly, will advertising be worth the money? While advertising is the most expensive form of getting the word out, used wisely and appropriately, it can be extremely effective.

Keep in mind the power of the Internet. Creating a Web site can be a form of publicity. You can reach an unlimited number of people. Your potential participants can access your information 24/7, and it can also be used as a one-stop resource for conference registration, accommodations, and air travel.

A Web site is a great promotional tool. It also demonstrates that you are up-to-date with new technology, but do not just put up a Web site for the heck of it. Make it easy to use, informative, and attractive with your message stated loud and clear. Use your Web site address in all of your promotional material.

~ Candy's Tips on Publicity ~

Getting the word out will be one of your top priorities. The person in charge of publicity has to be tenacious, charming, blessed with writing skills, and most important, be organized.

Magazines: Is there a magazine whose readers might attend your event? Contact them ASAP. Travel magazines and those published by auto clubs are also excellent targets. Since most have at least a three-month lead time, start early!

Events Column: If the newspaper has one, send them the basics: what is the event, the date(s), the time; mention a few highlights to grab interest; admission charge (if it is free, say so!); location and brief directions (for example, the Podunk Fairgrounds; take the Podunk exit off Route 66, and follow the signs). If possible include a phone number or e-mail for people to make contact for more info.

Features: If you have good pictures of a segment of your event and can write an accompanying story, send the Features Editor a query. Briefly explain your event, stating why you believe the magazine's readers would enjoy it, and offer to submit the story – again, months in advance! They may take you up on it!

Newspapers: Start contacting every newspaper within a 200-mile radius. (If your event is that special, yes they will come!) Learn the name, e-mail, and phone number of entertainment editors about six months in advance and keep in touch with them about every two or three weeks. Congratulate them on a feature that is related to your event and request guidelines for submitting press releases. Find out if they prefer e-mailed or faxed submissions. The reason for contacting them: newspaper people can come and go. This way if the original editor leaves, you will find out the name of the new one right away and still have a viable resource.

This is where writing skills are needed. Editors are very busy people; their reporters are frantically finishing last-minute articles on late-breaking news. Should you send them a well-written piece before their deadline, it is one less article they have to come up with and stands a very good chance of getting published.

TV: Even if your event is for only one day, after people see it on the 6 o'clock news, they will make note of it for next year! Get in touch with your local TV stations. This takes a real people-person, because you have to be persistent and upbeat all the time. Who is the man or woman who always shows up at events, telling viewers what a fun activity it is? That is the person you get in touch with. Try e-mailing or phoning them, and keep it up until you make contact. Tell them how much you enjoy their coverage of events! Then mention yours and give a few camera-worthy highlights. If your event has an admission fee, tell them they will of course get in free with their camera crew. Ask if they have some free time in the morning or afternoon and offer to come to the station to bring them some more information on the event—brochures and posters. If that is not possible, mail them a nice packet of data. If your event involves T-shirts, find out what size they wear and bring or send them one!

Here is a good strategy: should one of the local stations agree to cover your event, casually mention this to other stations as well, since you do not want them to miss out. No network affiliate likes to be scooped by a rival; if one shows up, the other just may come too. Make sure that all news crews are provided passes and assign someone with your event to be each one's guide. Suggest alternate points of interest so that they film different portions of the event.

THE INVITATION AND MARKETING MATERIAL

Your invitation and marketing media can include the registration form, ads, publicity, brochures, your Web site, e-mails, flyers, press releases, interoffice memos, posters, formal invitations, or even a phone call. There are hundreds of styles, shapes, sizes, colors, and even sounds that can be used to get your message out. This is time to get creative. Keep in mind your goals and objectives.

If your event is simple, you many need just the date, time, place, and objective. Come to the crab feed on Sunday the 13th at the boat club at 5 p.m., BYOB! RSVP required — call 555-1212.

But it can also be very complicated. You may need to create the brochure to convey the information about your event. If it is a professional event, make the brochure professional; if your event is whimsical and entertaining, make the material the same. If you work with a designer, be sure to communicate your intent and share the vision. With the ease of desktop publishing today, many people can design these materials themselves. Be sure to include all the pertinent information in your promotional material no matter what type of invitation. Can you imagine sending out 1,500 mailers without a time or location for the event? Even a misspelled name can be embarrassing. It could be a disastrous mistake. Read and re-read your material before it is printed.

To capture the reader's attention and solicit interest, use the following tips when creating your material.

- **Attention**: Attract the reader's attention! Use color, dramatic photos, over- or under-sized material, clever words, unusual paper, or interesting fonts.

- **Interest**: Offer a solution! The reader's interest is directly linked to a need or a desire. Offer the solution with a clearly stated understanding of their reward, such as education, a fun time, and a chance to meet like-minded people.

- **Desire**: State the benefits clearly. What's in it for them? The more benefits, the better.

- **Action**: Clear directions will make the reader take action. They may be in the form of commands such as, "Hold that date!" or "Call and register now!" Or "Mark your calendars now!"

- **Copy**: This is your sales pitch with benefits clearly outlined. Find a strong meeting title and descriptive subtitles. Provide pertinent meeting data: goals, objectives, registration information, the date, and times.

Use creative graphics. Whether it is a "save the date" postcard, a direct-mail brochure, or an e-mail blast; use colorful graphics to grab the attention of your attendees. For postcards, put slogans and graphics on both sides because there is a 50/50 chance the postcard will land face down on a desk. For e-mails, use a keyword in the subject line to prevent its being flagged as spam.

Event: Fundraiser

Location: Several piers on the San Francisco Bay

I was arranging for a 151-foot sailboat to dock at several ports around the San Francisco Bay. At each port, the public would board and take a trip with the crew around the Bay. Each trip was to raise awareness and money to support a journey from Hawaii to Pennsylvania via the Panama Canal. The ship was filled with young underprivileged boys on a vision quest. The best times that worked for the events were during low tides. At the last minute, before the scheduled times were about to be printed in the marketing material, we realized that the ship's hull was too deep for a couple of the piers. Fortunately we were able to reserve other piers with deeper water and change the times slightly to adjust for the tides. We had forgotten to check the tide chart!

Luckily, we were able to change the times and locations before the printed materials were sent out.

Anonymous

Putting Your Registration in the Invitation

Decide early on whether you want online or paper registration. If you have the capability to do the online registration, do it. It will save you a great deal of time and money. See in the back *References* section under

Management Resources for suggestions of online registrations software and companies who offer that service.

However, having a paper registration is still essential. With respect to collecting fees, get a system set-up right at the start.

Make sure the information in the registration form is clear and simple to interpret. Having to reimburse or collect more money is time consuming. Address the following in the registration form:

- Is payment required at the time of registration?

- Tell them how to make out the check.

- Do you accept credit cards? If so, be sure to have a place for the number and expiration date and a signature.

- Checks must be in U.S. dollars only.

- Cancellation policy. Under what conditions and at what date are there no refunds?

- Identify all costs above registration fee. For example, extra meals, excursions, or upgrades.

- Spell-out what the registration fee covers: breaks, reception, registration materials, meals, parking, airport transfers.

- Include specific instructions on how to register and when, and price savings if registering early.

- Tell them how they will receive their confirmation.

A couple of ways to attract more attendees is by announcing this information in your marketing and registration information. Using price reductions for multiple participants can bring your numbers up. To make it easier for organizations to send multiple attendees, give a discount for multiple registrations. Think of sliding discounts for every additional person after the first registrant. The first person pays full price, but if they send two, three, or more, the reduction kicks in.

Extend your early-bird rate. Build in some wiggle room for an early-bird rate, and as the date approaches, extend it by a few weeks. People are inclined to leap when they think they are getting a second chance.

DESIGNING YOUR WEB PAGE

One of the best marketing and promotional tools around today is Web sites. In several clicks of a mouse your potential customers can explore your event, find out all the details, and determine whether they want to register or buy what you are selling.

The easiest and fastest way a participant can register or buy tickets for your event is through your Web site. This means not only having a Web site but one that is easy to navigate and filled with all the appropriate information a participant may want. The site must provide all necessary data because you want them to register there and then.

Usability and effective communication are the most important factors in the success of your Web page. This includes making content easy to find and giving users everything they want. The easier it is for participants to find what they are looking for, the more people you will attract. Too often Web sites focus on looking attractive or quirky instead of understanding the true needs of customers. People are so busy today that they truly want straightforwardness and simplicity.

Online Registration

Registration used to require reams of paper, hours of database management, postage, sorting, and more paperwork. Today online registration has revolutionized the process and in doing so, increased customer service. Customers have 24/7 access to your Web site, can register, and get immediate confirmation. Once they are in the database, your keeping in contact with them is trouble-free, creating their name tag is a breeze, and creating the participant roster is simplified.

Money Saving Tips

- Use online registration.

- Design brochures and programs in-house. Give the printer a CD to eliminate proofreading and typesetting errors.

- Keep design and format to regular-sized paper. Odd-size brochures cost more to produce.

- Use bulk mail for large mailing. Make sure you have plenty of time for mail to arrive.

- Use technology when appropriate for marketing, registration, and normal communication.

- Check with the Convention and Visitor Bureaus for photos or artwork. They often lend them out at no charge.

REACHING YOUR TARGET MARKET

Whether your potential participants are individuals or groups of people, it is better to invite more people than to limit your marketing efforts. Use your marketing dollars wisely so that you can maximize profitability while effectively enticing prospects to attend. Consider:

- Who is your target audience?

- What business are they in?

- Which groups of people would be willing to pay to hear this information?

- Where are they?

- How do I find them?

- What is the best method to reach them?

Your intended participants should have the ability to pay and the desire to attend your event. Do not waste money on those outside your target market.

Search For Lists

There are hundreds of lists out there that are available for a fee. It may be the only way to get the appropriate lists you need. Make sure this expense is in your budget. Lists come from a number of places, from inside your business or rented from outside brokers. The lists come in the form of mailing labels or e-mail addresses. Each has pros and cons. Choose what works best for you and fits into your budget with the most impact.

NETWORKING FOR LEADS

There are many leads in any marketplace. After you have determined your target market, begin compiling leads that will fit their profile. The beginning of this process will be time-consuming but well worth your efforts.

The best way to gather leads is through your own personal set of connections. Begin by collecting all the business cards of everyone you meet. Get yourself out there and meet your connections. There are many organizations that you can tap into quickly and easily. Use local organizations, business associations, non-profit associations, chamber of commerce functions, or business clubs for networking.

Join these groups, attend their meetings and functions, and choose the group that is best aligned with your interests and the interests of the event. Just get involved and talk up your event. You will be surprised how helpful people will be as they become your best promoters. Remember to give out business cards and take as many as possible. Add these names to your database. You should start a database with your leads, using Excel or a good database program. You can use this database for future events as well. Also set up an e-mail list. Again, this will take time initially.

TIMING

Start early to lay your groundwork. Do what makes sense for your event. Some large organizations begin marketing years in advance. Some smaller events only need a few weeks or months, but try to get on people's calendars early. Being late with your promotions means poor attendance.

PROMOTING A GLOBAL EVENT

Marketing an event overseas can be demanding and challenging. Making your content and topics attractive to an international audience will be different from marketing stateside. International events can be one of the most rewarding aspects of your career and will open up a world of experiences for your faculty, visitors, and staff. Embrace the culture of the country where you are holding your event from the beginning.

What works in the United States will not necessarily work overseas. Plan your event with global awareness from the start. Integrate an on-site local advisory board and local facility into your program and use local key opinion leaders; they can be pivotal to raising awareness of your event and drawing participation. This is also a time to think about using a local destination management company for cultural guidance and direction.

Be very aware of the language you use when speaking and writing to your foreign co-workers, vendors, service providers, and participants. We Americans have thousands of creative catchy phrases, alliterations, puns, plays on words, or metaphors but they may not connect with a foreign audience or translate clearly.

Pay attention to your images, hand gestures, and symbols. They have vastly different meanings from one culture to another. We might take them for granted to mean one thing but they may be highly offensive to someone from another country. It might be a good idea to ask for assistance from local members before putting anything in writing. Also, ask your speakers, faculty, or entertainers to be aware of the translation differences.

Marketing tactics that work for one particular country may not for another. Every culture connects with key messages in a different way. Take the time to discover how your potential participants learn about events before you invest in your marketing tactics. For instance, mail service in Mexico City is not reliable; therefore, you want to market your event through the Internet rather than through a direct mail campaign. (Direct mail is not even used in Mexico as a marketing tactic.)

Be polite and mind your manners. The social aspect of events can be much more culturally important outside of the United States. You may find it challenging to stay within guidelines for meal expenditures. Also, pay careful attention to meal times. In Europe, if you plan a working lunch or allocate less than an hour for meals, you will be viewed as tactless. In Mexico, remember that people eat lunch around 4 p.m. If you try to schedule lunch at noon, people might perceive it as just a coffee break.

Each country has its unique culture, and the more homework you do to be aware of these distinctions, the better marketing material you will create, the more effective your promotion efforts will be, and the more appropriate the information you will share, hence, attracting more participants.

Lesson: Be mindful of language when visiting foreign countries.

I was working for an engineering association and one of our magazine covers that fall had George Bush on the cover. We blew it up and used it as a poster on our exhibit booth. The next month I was exhibiting at a conference in France and didn't think much about the artwork we were displaying. This was around the time that the United States was "renaming" French Fries "Freedom Fries" after France refused to support the Iraq War.

There was a huge exhibit hall, and some of the companies were based in France. You can imagine how many hateful words and glances ensued! I had to keep the artwork displayed; otherwise it would have shown just an empty display.

Luckily, the next day a friend of a friend arrived (who lived in France) to help me at the booth. She did not look French. She would translate everything that was said in my direction. Oh, the look on the French exhibitors faces when they found THAT out!

Ingrid

Visas Requirements in Flux

Keep attendees informed as much as possible of new rules and regulations and proper documentation they will need to follow for the event. Encourage them to continue to check the rules and laws before leaving the country because laws are subject to change. Perhaps give the participants the hosting country's embassy details for consultation. Because each country may have different admission requirements for nationals of different nations, it is very difficult for a sponsor to provide accurate information for every prospective attendee.

Gadgets, Contracts, and Security

Staying on Top of Technology

E vent planners use technology in so many areas of their business that it is critical to stay on top of changes. When used properly, technology can enhance communication, bring people together more effectively, dazzle the audience, improve the learning environment, and broaden the scope of meetings and events. Technology has made the process of bringing people together much easier and delivering the message more powerful.

It has become a large part of the event planning world. A technical innovation can be the computer with fast access and large memory, or it can be the way you use the Internet for research and promotion through Web sites, or the dynamic advancements in audio-visual equipment, Web casting and podcasting. An event planner must keep up with the latest technical developments.

Event planning is no longer a business for the technically challenged; just keeping up with the terminology is tricky. With the ever-increasing multi-functionality of gadgets and our hyper-connected culture, we need to be knowledgeable users. Do you use Web casting, video streaming, blogging, or podcasting yet? Do you belong to a virtual community? Or do you just get by with your simple e-mail functions and word processing application? It is a whole new world out there — get updated!

This chapter will bring you up-to-date on some of today's best technology. Improvements are being developed so fast that by the time you have read this chapter, something bigger, better, and faster will have hit the market. Either keep up or bring in a savvy tech person to help guide you.

KNOW WHAT YOU NEED

The first key to technology is being aware of what is available and knowing what you need for your particular event. One extra microphone can change your bottom line.

When technology plays a large role in your event, do a survey of the venue before signing any contracts. Meet with the network engineer or technical director and the venue's telecom manager for a tour. During the walkthrough, examine telecom closets and record the locations of jacks, wireless access points, and power drops. Itemize the cost of networking equipment such as routers, switches, and networked computers. Then examine the entire high speed Internet access (HSIA) connectivity agreement carefully and put prices, service, deliverables, and timetables in your contract.

TERMINOLOGY

Below are vocabulary and descriptions that you will encounter and ultimately need to know when you order technical equipment and services for your event. Take the following request at a hotel for example: "I will be requiring Internet capabilities via T1, DSL, or fiber circuit lines, all of which offer different bps rates or do you have wireless." There are so many different options that you need to know your requirements.

TECHNOLOGY TERMS	
Bandwidth	The data transmission capacity of an electronic line. It is expressed in bits per second (bps).

TECHNOLOGY TERMS	
Bps rate	Bits per second is a measure of the number of data bits (digital 0s and 1s) transmitted each second in a communications channel. This is usually in reference to modem speed.
DSL	DSL is short for digital subscriber line, which allows a modem to transform a plain telephone service line into a digital line and thus beef up bandwidth capability.
Fiber optic circuit	Data connectivity services for higher-bandwidth applications. It is a hair-thin glass strand designed for light transmission. It is capable of transmitting trillions of bits per second.
HSIA	High Speed Internet Access
ISP	Internet Service Provider
Kiosks	An interactive kiosk is an electronic communications tool that enables customers to serve themselves by accessing information, taking advantage of special offers, making purchases, or gathering information.
LAN	Local Area Network.
Podcasting	The distribution of audio or video files, such as radio programs, lectures and classes, or music videos over the Internet for listening on mobile devices (such as iPods) and personal computers.
Portable Media Player	A PMP is a handheld audio-video system that can record and playback from TV, DVD player, camera, or media file downloaded from Internet such as iPods, MP3 players, and other mobile devices.
RFID	Radio Frequency Identification Device uses access points to retrieve information remotely from special tags via radio waves. It captures data from up to 15 feet away. Used on name tags for tracking.

TECHNOLOGY TERMS	
Router	A router connects the T1 to an Internet Service Provider (ISP).
T1	A high speed Internet connection which is a dedicated copper circuit installed by the telephone company. Many hotels and other large venues are equipped with this service.
Teleseminar	A teleseminar is a telephone conference call. Attendees call into the teleseminar at a set time (not toll-free). The presenter calls in and begins their presentation. The advantage of attending a teleseminar is the ability to bring a group of people together from all over the nation from the comfort of your own home or office without the need for travel.
USB	Universal Serial Bus sends data to standard devices such as computers, but its popularity has prompted it to also become commonplace on video game consoles, PDAs, cell phones, and even devices such as televisions and home stereo equipment (mp3 players), and portable memory devices.
USB Flash Drives	Data storage devices integrated with a USB interface. They are typically small, lightweight, removable, and rewritable. USB flash drives have several advantages over other portable storage devices, particularly the floppy disk. They are generally faster, hold more data, and are considered more reliable than floppy disks.
Virtual Community	These communities are guaranteed to play a very important role in the future of the meetings industry. Technology will evolve to work better with virtual communities. The result of this symbiotic evolution is that virtual communities and the technology created to work with them will become the status quo, and those who reject these technological ideals and practices will be left behind.

TECHNOLOGY TERMS	
Web casting	The transmission of linear audio or video content over the Internet. A Web cast uses streaming media technology to take a single content source and distribute it to many simultaneous listeners and viewers.
Webinars	Similar to Web casting. Used to capture a recording to use for client support archives or for use as a saleable product.
Wireless	Internet wireless is a method of communication that uses low-powered radio waves to transmit data between devices. The term refers to communication without cables or cords, chiefly using radio frequency and infrared waves.

INTERNET ACCESS

Almost everyone in our society thrives on the Internet. For corporate and business events, having Internet access is a necessity. It may be through computer stations or kiosks or providing wireless service to the participants to use with their own laptops. When you need Internet access, decide how you will provide the service, how much bandwidth is necessary, how and where the computers will be set up, and how many you need. If you will be Web casting, choose your venue based on your Web cast needs. Not all hotels and venues are set up for your technology needs.

Where will the access points be placed - in the meeting rooms, around the community area of the venue, sleeping rooms, or all of the above? What kind of high speed access is needed? Is HSIA required in the meeting rooms for presentations? You must determine the requirements are for the planners, the participants, the presenters, and the vendors.

If a speaker needs to download presentations, slides, or graphics, the venue's T1 or DSL lines must be sufficiently fast and secure. Planners, of course, are able to order more or less bandwidth depending on the complexity of the meeting.

Many international, national, and regional hotels, motels, and resort chains are adding free Wi-Fi high speed Internet access as an amenity for guests and meeting planners. In addition to wireless in guest rooms, they offer access in a variety of public locations, such as lobbies, meeting rooms, restaurants, and lounges. Each site will vary. Find out where the access begins and ends. You may want your non-hotel guests to have access while they are attending your event as well.

Types of Bandwidth

T1 is the standard on-site HSIA available at most venues today. A switch then enables the T1 to be fractionalized or shared between meeting rooms via the venue's wiring. Venues that are not currently wired for T1 are able to secure temporary lines for clients, though they are expensive and time consuming to install.

Fiber offers the most capacity but is rare to find in most venues right now. Even though it is costly to install, it will become the standard for on-site HSIA in the near future. If you want the benefits of enormous capacity, lower cost, and more secure service now, find a venue with fiber optic circuit installed.

Inquire as to what is shared on the lines. If the hotel's sleeping rooms share the bandwidth with your meeting rooms, you can have a significant deceleration right in the middle of an important presentation or when doing other vital work such as printing badges, handling registration, or updating the latest spreadsheet. If the hotel does not budge on allocating a full T1 line to you, then consider hiring an outside IT company or have the hotel create a DSL line to get a dedicated non-sharing circuit.

The Cost of Access

Know the going rates and what is negotiable for Internet connectivity. It is recommended that when deciding on effective technology, planners get technical advice from information technology (IT) experts who specialize in digital events. It is crucial that every planner have a working knowledge of technology costs after decisions are made with the IT expert, the venue, or the outside technical consultant.

Internet access can be an expensive portion of your event. If you know the approximate costs, you can negotiate with confidence with your venue and save money. To negotiate be prepared with a lower amount competitive venues are charging, or the fact that others offer more service for the same price, or their staff is more educated, or they are willing to give something complimentary. Of course, it is understood and respected that a venue needs to be compensated and make revenue, but there is a difference between that and price gouging a naive meeting planner.

Event: Annual Sales Conference
Duration: 3 Days
Participants: 2,500
Venue: Large Chain Hotel

When negotiating with the hotel they wanted to charge $1,500 per meeting room for high-speed Internet access with T1 lines. The cost would have totaled $12,000 since the client wanted eight rooms and ten computers. This sounded outrageous and a bit unethical. After some homework and negotiating we were able to come to a conclusion to save money and still receive the service we needed. The venue agreed to create a local area network (LAN) and use one T1 line (worth $2,000) and connect the other rooms to that T1. We offered to pay $4,000 ($500 per room) and requested the hotel IT staff to do the switching, and we paid an additional $2,000 for the T1 line. With a little knowledge and homework we were able to save an enormous amount of money for our client.

Kathleen Currey, Corporate Meeting Planner
San Francisco, CA

PODCASTING

Podcasting and the technologies associated with it are custom-made for meeting professionals. Digitally recorded podcasts are enhanced versions of the audio tape recording. Because they are high quality, they can be used by organizations and associations to distribute information to members who are unable to attend the meeting. Podcasts are easily downloaded from your Web site.

When is podcasting good for business? When you have a Web site, a digital audio recording, and an audience wanting your content, you have the key components to podcast. Podcasting distributes content to people who want the information in a format they can easily use. As long as they have Internet access, the audience can be anywhere in the world. It even allows the participant to listen to the information at their leisure.

Podcasting can function as a revenue generator or a value-added feature for clients and attendees. In the days of analog recording, conference attendees would buy audio tapes of sessions. The sound quality was usually poor and the fast-forward and rewind features made it difficult to isolate the content that was really needed. All that has changed with podcasts, the sound is impeccably clear and navigating through the material is simple.

A bonus is that you can include visuals such as slides or video from a session and additional content such as background information about the speaker that audio tape recordings just cannot provide. The digital format allows users to create their own experience with the media by picking and choosing what content they want to use. Users are younger and more tech-savvy than ever, and they have high standards when it comes to digital media.

USING KIOSKS

There is a growing public awareness of value-added services of kiosks that are everywhere today. You find them at airports, hotels, and when you pick up your rental car. You see them at the bank, in the supermarket, and in your local mall. National parks, libraries, post offices, and other government agencies use kiosks. They are becoming very a common technology in our daily lives.

What are they and how are they being used in the event planning arena? They are being used at large convention centers, hotels, trade shows, conferences, sporting events, festivals, and concerts. They can enhance your event by delivering a welcome message and information, providing local entertainment and sightseeing details, publishing promotions, providing travel information by supplying airline links, providing exhibitor and booth information, offering coupons, and displaying and updating agendas.

NETWORKING WITH TECHNOLOGY

At conference and conventions for the last half century, we have identified one another through our name badges. Now something has come along to replace them. The days of staring at someone's chest or belly (if the badge is on a lanyard) may be over. We now have the radio frequency identification device (RFID).

The RFID is not the best solution yet, but a step in the right technological direction. There is a handheld wireless device that will tell me, for instance, who is within five feet of me. The participants who uploaded a photo and data will appear on the screen. It also contains the entire participant list and you can set your radar to beep when you come close to a person you have highlighted. Besides the great networking possibilities, it also offers event agenda updates, surveys your participants, and gives sponsors space for promotions. The price is $30 to $40 per attendee per day but sometimes offered at the expense of sponsors.

THE NEW BREED OF AUDIO-VISUAL SERVICES AND EQUIPMENT

Fast forward from yesterday's standard audio-visual equipment such as microphones, overhead projectors, LCD projectors and the like, and you find a new breed of technology available for business, educational meetings, social, and special events. It is important to keep up with what is available and understand how to use it to enhance your events. Today it is much more than lights, camera, and action.

Whether the event is inside or outdoors, your technology needs can range from a single flipchart to a multi-media extravaganza using state-of-the-art equipment. When it is more than a flipchart, the event can require dozens of vendors involved in set-up, and installation can be extensive and time-consuming.

Business and Educational Meetings

Technology is evolving at supersonic speeds, enhancing the event and meeting industry and increasing the adaptability of event communications. A few of the newer tools are: presentation management, Web casting, audience response system, video conferencing and RFID. Using any of these tools in addition to your standard audio-visual equipment can boost your participants' ability to communicate effectively and maximize the success of your event.

Presentation management is a service that directs the electronic presentation materials for educational sessions, training meetings, or any other event where multiple presenters are involved. Speakers submit their electronic presentations in advance via a secure Web site or on-site at the speaker-ready room. Presentations are electronically transmitted to the speakers' assigned session room, streamlining meetings by allowing planners to control the computer and audio-visual equipment used in meeting rooms. Presenters no longer need to bring their own computers, eliminating equipment compatibility issues, and once the presentations are collected in one central location, they can be easily assembled for Web casting, podcasting or educational purposes after the event.

Web casting services provide a powerful and progressive addition to live events by expanding the audience and enhancing the program even for those in attendance. Events can be streamed live or archived for later viewing in audio only or audio-video formats. Registration options capture relevant information about viewers as well as prevent unauthorized access to content by requiring viewers to enter a password to view the event.

Audience Response System (ARS) offers interactive database programs that produce instant reports from live input. ARS enhances an event by involving the audience and offering a quick method to gather valuable information. They can streamline complex voting procedures. Participants are given individual keypads and can answer multiple-choice questions or cast votes in real time, with results being tabulated and displayed moments later.

Video conferencing presents an opportunity to have meetings without having to travel. The benefits inspire people to communicate more effectively and more efficiently and ultimately makes organizations more productive. Besides saving time, it also decreases cost, reduces travel time, encourages collaboration, and stimulates communication.

Radio frequency identification devices (RFID) are being used by meeting planners for a number of reasons such as session control access, continuing education unit tracking, crowd flow tracking, traffic pattern reporting, and post-show demographic analysis.

These are but a few of the options available for your events. Speak with professional production companies or your specific venue for all available choices. Ask about satellite conferencing, Internet presentation and archiving, video production and presentation playback, interactive theater, and other interesting methods of enhance your event.

Social and Special Events

The design of your audio-visual and technology needs begins with concepts taken from the defined vision of the event. From there, sketches and renderings, floor plans, and schematics are created, designating where everything — stage lights, video, computer projection equipment, scenery, and the portable rest rooms—will be placed. The design will derive from client meetings as well as hotel or venue site evaluations, show and room limitations, electrical specifications, and your goals and objectives.

Your objective might be to promote your message clearly in a beautiful and artistic manner while impressing and winning over your audience. Or do you want to blast your audience out of their seats, wow them, and keep them talking long after the meeting has ended? Will you need fireworks? Laser lights? Theatrics? Or how about indoor state-of-the-art computer-controlled, intelligent lighting? Or do you just want the best lighting and sound for an outdoor birthday bash? Whatever you want, it is probably available no matter how remote the location.

The mark of a professional event planner is that all aspects of your events run flawlessly, avoiding the most visible and annoying failure technology—and that means bringing in the best staff and professional technicians. They will install, maintain, and operate all kinds of production equipment so that every detail is accounted for, right down to duct taping the cable to the floor.

Contracts and Insurance

It is likely you will be signing different types of contracts during the course of planning your event, one for the facility and sleeping rooms, another for food and beverage, one for audio-visual equipment, one for transportation services, airline or rental car services, others for your speakers, entertainers, the tent company, or a catering business.

Insurance is an increasing necessity in the world of event planning. There are many ways to insure an event, and many of your vendors will require you to have insurance and be named on the insurance certificates as additionally insured.

About Contracts

A contract is an understanding of what is expected of both parties and how to resolve any problems that arise. They present an opportunity to get some challenging questions answered before the work begins. A contract will set a tone for cooperation and will define the parameters of your ongoing working relationship. Your contract should include a clear work plan with specific deliverables tied to specific dates. A good contract will include much of the following:

- Title.

- Brief description of the event.

- Brief description of the services or equipment needed.

- Detailed list of the services to be provided with projected dates of delivery.

- Who is responsible for what parts of the project? (contractor, subcontractors, staff)

- What are the expectations for communicating the progress of the project?

- Payment schedule and amounts.

- Clarity on expenses   hourly rates versus fixed pricing.

- Ownership of the work products.

- How conflicts will be resolved.

- How parties can void the contract.

- Proper signatures.

To protect everyone involved, everything should be confirmed in writing. Contracts have become more detailed and complicated. The days of hand shakes and cocktail napkin agreements are long gone. You would be wise to find counsel who is up-to-date on specific contract information.

Contracts are negotiated with the understanding if your mutual needs and goals are entered into with a mutual commitment; they are created to be fair to both parties. Some may be a simple one or two page document, say for a speaker or vendor, or they can be lengthy and complex with comprehensive terms and conditions as with a conference center or hotel.

Remember to sign the contract as a representative of your company or organization, especially important if you are a hired independent contractor. Sometimes you are the one and only so you must study the fine print before signing. Everything is negotiable in a contract as long as both parties are in agreement.

CREATING A CONTRACT

After two parties have entered into a written agreement (a contract) the terms control their obligations. It is important to get all the commitments written down because if a dispute arises, a judge or arbitrator will require both parties to perform what is in the contract. Oral agreements cannot be enforced. Get it in writing!

The contract typically begins when signed by both parties. The ending date can be changed if it contains a clause stating that the term of the contract can be shortened.

The contract should reflect the payment terms. Ideally for the group, no payments should be made until after the program, except a deposit. The contract also should state that final payments are contingent upon receiving a final, itemized invoice from the company.

AMENDING A CONTRACT

Amending contracts is common practice, but follow appropriate procedures. Avoid handwritten changes if at all possible since they may be difficult to read and may be disputed if they were not properly validated by each party or if it is tricky to tell whether both parties signed after the notes. Legally they may not be accepted.

If the amendment is small or minor, make notes of the changes in the margins of the contract, initial, and date them. Return the contract so that changes can be included in the next revised version. It is also a good idea to write a cover letter with requested changes listed and attach a newly amended contract. With today's technology making a fully corrected copy without handwritten changes and signed by both parties is incredibly easy. That is the ideal contract. If changes are significant an addendum can be incorporated into the contract.

EXPECT THE UNEXPECTED

After a contract becomes valid and binding, a breach of contract occurs if one party cancels or does not fully perform its obligations. The other party is entitled to compensation for losses. Termination of the contract occurs when either or both parties cancel a contract. There are several legal reasons for contract termination. Two common ones are called "act of god" and "force majeure." Two things must occur under each of these principles, an unexpected event that makes performance of the contract illegal or impossible.

ACTS OF GOD AND FORCE MAJEURE

The September 11 attacks and Hurricane Katrina are recent examples of acts of god and forces majeure, but sometimes the lines are not so defined. Here are some examples where termination is allowed but damages are expected:

- **A change in economic circumstances**: Dot com bust and the downturn of the economy were not reasons for termination.

- **Greater Expense**: When fewer participants will be attending than previously expected, obligations of contract will require the same amount of money to be expended.

- **Labor Issues**: These can be related to strikes, boycotts, or picket lines. For example, when Colorado passed anti-gay legislation and when Arizona did not adopt the Martin Luther King holiday, many groups wanted to pull their conferences and conventions. Contracts obliged them to stay or lose in damages. Cancellations are acceptable, yet termination is not. Any venue under contract would have the right to seek damages for the cancellation.

- **Fear of Travel**: Threats of terrorism, political upheaval, and contagious outbreaks are not a cause for cancellation because they are not forces majeure or acts of god.

- **Threat of Anything**: Terrorism and economic or political reasons are not cause for terminations. They do not fall in either category.

As you can see, lawyers should define contract language about your obligations, but if you do not have a lawyer, here are some issues to watch for and ideas that can save you time and trouble with contracts. Remember, good contracts protect both parties. Pay close attention to what you are signing. Use these tips and ideas for everyone you deal with and for all contracts you are negotiating.

- Always sign a contract as an agent on behalf of your company or the company that hired you. You do not want to be held personally responsible.

- Look for clearly stated dates, rates, intentions, names, contacts, and numbers (hotel rooms, meals, and exhibitors).

- Always read every word in the contract. It is amazing how many people have not read a whole contract before signing it. Do not be penny-wise and pound-foolish.

- Pay attention to cut-off dates. Keep in regular contact with suppliers even after the contract is signed.

- Ask for a clause in the contract that states that any fees not in the contract will not be applicable to your group.

- Never sign a contract unless you agree with it in its entirety. Cross out or edit clauses with which you do not agree, initial them, and get the supplier to initial his or her agreement.

- Make sure that the cancellation clause is reciprocal. Contract offers are inherently one-sided   it is your job to balance it out.

- Specify the dates and times in the contract, i.e.: "The cut-off date for sleeping room reservations is Saturday June 28, 2007, at 5 p.m." instead of "The cut-off date is 30 days before the meeting."

- Make sure that all associated fees are stipulated in your contract.

- Include all tax and gratuity percentages in your contract. Understand what they are and how to calculate them.

- Negotiate attrition into your contract for rooms, food, and beverage. Ask that attrition be calculated at their profit, not the full rates. If the hotel can pick up the rooms, negotiate that no attrition fee be necessary.

- Cancellation and attrition fees should be based on the meeting site's lost profit not lost revenue. This can be 70 percent to 80 percent for guest rooms and 30 percent to 40 percent for food and beverage.

VENUES, AUDIO-VISUAL, FOOD, BEVERAGE, AND MORE

The next few guidelines should be taken into consideration when you sign a contract with vendors and suppliers. You can replace the word hotel or venue with the audio-visual company, the caterer, or the tent company. You will be signing contracts with all of these vendors so that you must pay attention and read them thoroughly. If you have a lawyer, let her read them.

Conduct preliminary negotiations with the hotel or venue before spending money on a site inspection. Ask to see their typical contract before you visit. Make sure that it meets your requirements or be prepared to negotiate. Add to the contract any amendment that you want covered for your event. Negotiations can begin early enough that if there is a real problem and a solution is impossible, you will have saved travel time, and your bids will be more accurate.

When dealing with the hotel on any additions to the contract, make sure you are speaking with the person who can make those decisions, but know what you are willing to negotiate and what you will not. Ask for everything and be prepared to compromise.

Let them know that you are looking at several properties or vendors. They may be more willing to make some deals. If you really want a specific venue, establish a good relationship with the sales staff.

Go over the final contract with your sales person as well as your in-house attorney (of course). Take a few days to sign the contract. If you make changes, try to get an original with all the changes included. Clarity is good! Make sure everything is in writing.

The contract should address which entity is responsible for the safety and security of the audio-visual equipment. Ideally, it should be the audio-visual company. The event planner should not accept responsibility for stolen or damaged equipment.

Hidden Agendas – Privacy Concerns

After you have chosen your site, be aware of the policies regarding your participants' information. The last thing you want is your attendees' getting unsolicited mail from outside vendors and services because the hotel or venue sold their information. Watch for statements and or clauses in the contract that say that the hotel reserves the right to disseminate the members' information to third parties for any lawful or business purpose and watch for added provisions to indemnify them from any liabilities resulting from the use of the information.

Sometimes they may ask for permission that is provided to the federal government for national security purposes. A certain amount of information will have to be released for the vendors and third parties to conduct business but knowing where the information can be distributed is important. Negotiate in the contract the right to approve all uses of the participants' information.

SIGNING FOREIGN CONTRACTS

U.S. contractual agreements include standard industry assumptions that are not necessarily relevant in other countries. Discuss with the vendors and suppliers those things that we take for granted, such as whether the meeting space in your hotel is free of charge when a certain number of rooms are booked or what does a coffee break mean in their county? And of course, put everything in writing.

You and the other party must agree on the language and currency you will be using and whose law to use for dispute resolution, yours or theirs? Designating a governing language avoids disputes when different language versions of a contract conflict because of the translation. Choosing an official currency protects the parties against value fluctuations that can affect event pricing. Depending on the country, the court system may be efficient or slow. Without an agreement on which country's laws will apply in a dispute, both sides may try to resolve the matter in their own courts, causing confusion and delay.

There should be a carefully worded clause to cover all unanticipated and unavoidable incidents that would cause cancellation, including civil unrest, terrorism, and major airline strikes. Planners should not cede control over declaring a force majeure cancellation to the meeting facility; local hosts are far less likely to cancel a meeting than the planner. For example, terrorism in the United States would probably not cause a meeting venue in Britain to cancel, but it might prevent the attendees from getting onto the airplane. In situations where there are differing opinions on what constitutes a force majeure, the best option is to create a mechanism for consultation and mediation if a dispute arises.

INSURANCE

Unfortunately, people are litigious. Events of all kinds face the risk of lawsuits. Planners should understand and protect their events against potential losses and lawsuits by having a basic knowledge of insurance issues affecting them, the organization they work for, and their clients. It is unwise to take the risk of being unprotected. Large and small events are complex financial propositions involving intimidating financial liabilities. Whether you purchase event insurance depends on how important the event is to your corporation financially, what kind of financial risk you are assuming, and that many municipalities and venues will not reserve your space without a certificate of insurance.

The odds of your event's being cancelled are not great, but when something does happen and you have a loss, it will probably be significant. So considering all of the dangers out there, both natural and the willful actions of others, you need to secure insurance for your next big meeting or special event.

Types of Insurance

Insurance companies will consider the type of event you are holding, the number of participants attending, the location, and your level of risk and exposure. For instance, you will pay more for insurance if you are holding a tractor-pull versus a craft show.

There is a public entity type of insurance that covers events such as a group of citizens wanting to hold a July Fourth block party with street closures, a spiritual group holding a service in a public park, or a parade, street fair, sidewalk sale, wedding, or reunion. There is even wedding cancellation insurance.

Look into all the insurance opportunities and determine what works best in your situation. Here are some insurance categories that you might need: general liability, event cancellation, promoter liability, participant legal liability coverage, liquor liability, third-party property damage, participant and spectator medical benefits, weather, flood, earthquake, automobile, boiler and machinery, directors and officers, participant legal liability (sporting events only), accidental death and dismemberment, spectator and participant medical, hired and non-owned automobile liability, hired and non-owned automobile physical damage, third party property damage, rental equipment, and unlimited certificates of insurance, including special certificates.

Here is a small list of things that can go wrong and why you should protect yourself. This is not a scare tactic by any means—just a reality check.

- Adverse weather conditions disrupting travel or affecting outdoor activities.

- Union strikes causing disruption of travel services or venue staffing and services.

- Speakers or entertainers who fail to show for whatever reason.

- Venue damage by fire or storm.

- Venue not available because the owner double booked.

- The failure of essential production resources such as the power supply.

- Terrorism that causes security alerts, disrupting travel or diverting flights.

- An outbreak of infectious diseases leading to a quarantine control or restricted travel.

- Eruption of civil disorder, revolution, war, or other political catastrophes.

- Sudden political events such as coups or disputes with other countries causing border closures or withdrawal of visa facilities.

- Delay and disruption of travel arrangements. What happens if you have a group stranded at the airport by bad weather? Who pays for the unused food, drink, and accommodation?

- Property damage—your own or property belonging to the venue or site.

- Loss of enjoyment and motivation—reduction in quality for participants.

- Reduced attendance due to some unforeseen event, leading to loss of revenue—potentially devastating for events staged for-profit.

- Loss of reputation. It may be necessary to incur expenses to preserve the reputation of the event for next time.

Type of Event: Luncheon to celebrate a ground breaking
Duration: 2 hours
Number of Attendees: Booked for 200; set-up for 240
Type of Venue: Construction-site for new medical clinic
Subject of Story: One of the hosts murdered during event
Murder weapon: My cream of chicken soup

The event went flawlessly until people lined up to shake hands with the new owners of the land. Then a "disruptive element" arrived.

A parent of a patient, a child who had been disfigured accidentally by the doctor, appeared and started a fight with the doctor, repeatedly pushing the doctor's head into my pot of chicken soup. The doctor had his trachea and lungs so badly burned by hot soup that he died on his way to the hospital.

Needless to say, the event was cancelled by the investigating officers, but I did get paid. A big problem was the police held the equipment I had on-site until they finished with the crime scene. The defense attorneys demanded that the banquet remain set until the trial was over.

I was just starting in business and all my serving assets were in that hall, including my folding tables (40), stacking chairs (240), my chafers, utensils, dinnerware, everything. I was essentially out of business until the trial was over. It was only ten weeks later when they released my equipment; it could have put me out of business.

Solution: My business insurance salesman was my brother-in-law. Before I opened my doors, he insisted I be insured against just about everything, including losing the use of my business assets due to a catastrophic event.

Luckily, all the necessary equipment from the vendors I did business with rained in within five working days. I fulfilled most of my contracts. For a while I had to use the ugliest, cheapest chafers until the manufacturer finally shipped the replacements I ordered—the day before the court released my equipment.

My old on-site equipment became the property of the insurance company, but they sold it back to me for a pittance because they did not want to go to the trouble of auctioning it off. Instead they came up with a fair price and sold it back to me.

Lesson learned:

A) Always have good insurance.

B) Every knock is a boost. The police and prosecutors ate my food while they did the primary investigation, and afterwards I got increased business from official county and city events, many weddings, and "Sweet 16" parties for the families of the police department and coroner's staff.

C) No news is bad news: I tripled my catering business within a year. The publicity about a guest drowning in my soup brought the morbidly curious to my doors that I turned into catering sales by generous samplings of our wares. My retail bakery sales quadrupled.

D) Pick my suppliers more carefully. An equipment vendor who will not produce in an emergency is worthless.

E) Always listen to my brother-in-law.

Dr. Andrew A. Gryffindor IV, PhD.
Retired

Security Issues

afety precautions are a serious matter. Global events have increased our need for security, which has touched almost every facet of the event planning process. We now need security for crowd control at a large concert or sporting event, for guarding a high profile person, securing venues, the personal belongings of the participants, or a public area for an event. Today more than ever your personal data are at risk. Security measures are extremely important for protecting personal information, your network, and your personal computer.

Now we must deal with metal detectors, IDs of the tangible and the ethereal kind, passwords, personal body guards for special guests, and intensive security for large events. Security has always been an event planner's concern, but it was usually a hidden activity. Today, planners are looking to the property's director of security and general manager for guidance and assistance.

The price of security today can come with a hefty price-tag. Be sure to budget appropriately.

PROTECTING YOUR HIGH PROFILE GUESTS

Prominent figures in our society must take extra precautions even when stepping out their front door. When they go to a public event, tight security is very present and required for their safety. Many different types of people fall into the category of "high security" stature. It is best to understand who will need extra security and who does not. If you are not sure, ask them.

When your event includes people who require extra security, hiring the best is imperative as well as knowing your role in maintaining everyone's safety.

Celebrities may have their own bodyguards but will expect you to provide some additional security if they are coming to perform. If your event includes celebrity guests, they may be more willing to come if you offer additional on-site security. It is one thing to provide security inside a venue but in the crowd outside, fans can get overly excited and rush the person entering the venue.

Political figures also require protection. The level of security required will depend on their stature. Usually political figures' protection is handled through the government, but it is important to ask either the politician or someone in their office. Remember, when you are working with the Secret Service or the State Department, you are under their orders. If they say they will arrive at this time and enter from this direction, that is what they will do and you must deal with it.

Sports personalities run the same risks as celebrities, and like celebrities, they often travel in an entourage with security, but always ask to be on the safe side.

Even private citizens are at risk if they go public with controversial opinions. Adversarial people need protection too. Know when to hire help.

When high-security public figures have private security staying overnight, take room blocks and assignments into consideration. They may request a suite or several connecting rooms to be blocked off. If this is the case, alert hotel security so that they can work together to build a layout with exits and evacuation plans.

When using a private security company, give them as much advance notice as possible. They will want to do their own survey of the venue and all the streets leading up to it. Security should be left to professionals.

CROWD CONTROL—SECURITY

When crowds are large, it is very likely that security will be necessary. Helping guests feel secure at special events is vital today, and the larger the crowd, the better the security needs to be. When producing large special events or events with celebrities, do not scrimp on costs associated with security personnel. With that said, communication becomes very critical.

When planning for crowd control or security, take into consideration how many people are expected, the age of the audience, and the reason they are there. Compare a large crowd of 20-somethings gathering for a hip hop concert versus a crowd of 30-somethings coming together for a church revival. The needs for security will be vastly different. How about alcohol? Will it be served? Will the audience be drinking or doing recreational drugs? These are very important questions, and the answers need to be passed on to security protecting the event.

DATA SECURITY

Failure to protect personal information can have serious repercussions, from fines and penalties levied by credit card companies to lawsuits and damaged reputations. The Sarbanes-Oxley Act (SOX) has created a responsibility for people with access to data to take measures to keep them confidential. Under SOX, that responsibility spreads to outside meeting planners, hotels, convention venues, and anyone who handles the data of your participants. Meeting planners can no longer assume that their computers and cyber networks will be safe from information theft; they need to verify that safeguards are in place.

When confidential information exists in an on-site meeting network or in a registration database, it is the planner's responsibility to protect it. To minimize risk and liability, meeting professionals need high standards of due diligence.

REGISTRATION DATA

You must take steps to protect personal data your attendees will be giving you when registering for your event. If you are using online registration make sure your connection is using the Secure Sockets Layer (SSL) encryption protocol. (The URLs for Web sites with an SSL connection begin with https instead of http.) The data should be stored in an encrypted, relational database behind a firewall to prevent unauthorized access.

Registration forms, housing lists, and other hard copies with confidential information should never be faxed, given freely to staff, volunteers, or the venue personnel, or be left in the open. Staffers with access to this information should have shredders at their desks.

When a third-party vendor has been hired for on-site registration, do not send the pre-registration database via e-mail. Use a secure File Transfer Protocol site where the file can be downloaded. When you select outside vendors, ask about their data security practices. Decide who is authorized to access the data and how that access is controlled. Be sure the contract includes language that makes it clear that you own the data, and that they may not be shared without permission.

Using intelligent data handling policies and well-designed contracts with hotels and other third parties can go a long way toward protecting personal registration data. Negligent or careless practices can mean that personal information may be used in unexpected ways or worse— exposed to theft. Privacy policies and practices are not enough to reduce your exposure to risk. When you contract with third parties, include a contract clause that passes along the responsibility for safeguarding confidential information. It can state that any data that we give you belongs to us and are confidential. You cannot use them for any purpose other than the purpose for which we are giving them to you. When the contract is complete, the data must be returned.

WHAT IS YOUR PRIVACY POLICY?

A privacy policy tells people how you will use their information. According to TRUSTe, the Federal Trade Commission's Fair Information Practices are the closest thing to a standard for online privacy protection. Based on the principle of full disclosure, they include:

- **Notice**: Disclose what information is collected and how it will be used. When you collect the information you must advise the person that their information might be shared and get their permission to do so.

- **Choice**: Allow people to choose how their information is used. Some people will choose to allow their data to be given and used by third parties such as hotels or airlines.

- **Access**: Allow people to review the information once they have disclosed it. This allows them to go back and look at or edit any information given you.

- **Security**: Secure personal information so that it stays private.

- **Redress**: Enable people to resolve any problems that arise.

If that information is compromised by a security breach or carelessness you must notify the people whose information was exposed.

The need for data security does not end when the event ends. Be sure that suppliers return confidential data within a reasonable time. When you no longer need this information, erase it completely. Scrub or wipe your hard drive.

NETWORK PROTECTION

Corporations, organizations, companies, and associations spend plenty of money with their own security in their offices. They should request the same level of security when using an off-site venue. When using network access at venues it is extremely important to have protection from intrusion. It is recommended that you ask your network services provider about how the network is protected against denial of service attacks and other intrusions. Make sure there is a network operations control center with intrusion detection and incident response capabilities. All network servers should be in a room with restricted access. If you have complex networking needs, bring IT support or contract a reliable on-site provider.

If security for your participants' computer access is important, do not rely on public wireless access as it can expose your participants to possible data theft. You can provide an SSID or service set identification number that restricts access to event participants. For the highest level of security, ask for a Wi-Fi Protected Access (WPA) compliant network that encrypts the data. To gain access, each user needs a unique password.

On-Site Logistics

Logistically Speaking

*T*here are dozens of details to handle in the months before your event. During that time, winding up all the particulars is a non-stop process requiring good organizational skills. One misstep can make or break an event. This is the most crucial time involving the timelines and checklists you created and have been following. Get them back out, revise them, create more checklists, and assign the ones you have to the appropriate people—whatever it takes to get the job done in the most efficient manner.

For example, when you have a good idea of the number of participants registering for your event, relay the number to all involved parties including vendors and suppliers. You will be talking to the facility, caterers, set-up people, decorators, speakers, musicians, security team, volunteers, and maybe your participants—all who are involved in the event.

A couple of weeks before the event you should start compiling the event materials, making copies of handouts, printing name tags, making lists of all kinds, confirming travel and transportation, boxing and shipping materials to the site. You will be making your signs and posters and shipping them, too.

You also need to prepare for the days of the event by creating checklists, refining schedules and confirming everything with every player involved. Begin making copies of all important paperwork such as your contracts, permits, rooming lists, menus, names, and phone numbers of everyone involved. These items will be your reference material and will ultimately go into your binder to share with your right hand assistant or other planners. When problems and issues arise, and they will, you will have all the information in one place for reference. The binder should be so organized that if you just handed it off to someone else, that person could run the show without you.

FINALIZING THE DETAILS

NOTE: We cannot possibly list everything you need to do in the weeks before your event, but we have listed some important steps in the pages that follow. If you have been making and using your checklists and timelines, you should be way ahead of the game.

Registration Confirmation

There are many ways registration confirmation can be handled. If you decided early on to purchase a pre-packaged registration software application, confirmations were probably immediately sent to the participants when they registered. If this is the case, download and print the information.

If you did not use a pre-packaged application, you probably entered the names and information into a database. Print out and review the information. This database will be used for sending confirmations, creating name badges, and creating a participant list. Generate your database in an appropriate program for storing this type of information.

All confirmations should go out as soon as registrations are received to alleviate a mass mailing just before the event. Participants want to know well in advance that they have a confirmed reservation so that they can block the time out in their calendars and begin making travel arrangements.

Confirm With Speakers and Entertainment

Confirm with your speakers their needs for audio-visual, room set-up, transportation, and any special requirements or requests. Know when they are arriving and how they are getting to the site. Is a volunteer picking them up from the airport, is there a shuttle bus, or will they be taking a cab or renting a car? Make sure their room is reserved at the hotel. Have a copy of their presentation materials. Ask for any last-minute changes.

Confirm with your entertainers their needs for audio-visual equipment, staging, and transportation. Know when they are arriving and how they are getting to the site. Will they be needing transportation to the facility or will they arrive on their own? Will they need sleeping rooms? Will they join the group for meals? Ask for any last minute changes.

Confirm the set up of all of your venue space. Make sure the rooms are big enough for your latest estimated number of participants and downsize if necessary. Are the seating arrangements still appropriate and conducive for each particular event?

Go over the audio-visual requirements and food and beverage orders with the site personnel and caterers. Find out if your block of hotel rooms is being picked up. If it is not, let go of some of the rooms. Keep in touch with your site and vendors the few weeks before the event.

Arrange For Pre-Event Meeting

Hold a pre-event meeting the day or evening before the event with the facility and staff. Invite all department heads of the facility to this meeting—the general manager, the directors of food and beverage, audio-visual and technology director, security, housekeeping, banquet room, and maybe the chef. Invite the vendors if necessary. Review the event resume, rooming lists, food and beverage, audio-visual requests, and room set-up. Discuss any last-minute details or changes. Let them know who has purchasing power when audio-visual or food is needed at the last minute. Get the cell, pager, or extension numbers for everyone and the hours of their availability. Know whom to call when something breaks, the room is too hot or too cold, or the break food has not been delivered. Go over everything. This may be your last opportunity to get it right!

Finalize Transportation Needs

Who needs a ride? Are all your airline tickets purchased? Do you need all those buses you hired or do you need to request more? Who is picking up whom at the airport? Does the hotel shuttle need to run more often because your numbers have increased? Are the limousines confirmed? Check to make sure everything is covered in this department.

Contact Vendors and Suppliers

If you are using outside vendors, suppliers, and multiple venues and sites, initiate an ongoing dialogue with them as to your needs and wants. As the number of participants rises or decreases, each supplier will need to be informed, whether it is the caterer, the hotel, the bus company, or the T-shirt maker, correct numbers are essential for them to do their job well. If you are ordering flower arrangements for 100 tables, and the numbers change so that only 50 tables are needed, the florist needs to know as soon as possible This is true for every item that will be used. It will also reveal any bits and pieces you forgot to order.

Event: Wedding

Lucy is 18 years old and a captain for a catering company. When she and her boss went over the details of the wedding that she would coordinate, the one detail she could not handle was ordering the champagne because she was underage. Her boss said he would take care of it and told her the champagne would be delivered to the bride's father and he would sign for it. At the reception, the bride's father came up to her and said they were ready for the champagne toast. Lucy went to find the champagne and could not find it. She went to the bride's father and asked if it had been delivered. He said no. So Lucy had to ask her employees if anyone was 21 and if they had a credit card. Luckily enough one young woman, barely 21 herself, had a credit card. Lucy sent her the local store for champagne. The day was saved. Lucy found out later that her boss forgot to order the champagne. How many 18-year-olds can think that fast? A true event planner!

Jerry, Event Planner
San Francisco

Create Event Binder

This is a binder for you, the event planner, and any other person who will be working closely with you. It will contain the documents that are the blueprint for the entire event and will be your safety net. You cannot possibly keep all the information in your head. Put it all in one place, your binder, so you know where everyone and everything is at any given time.

Creating lists for this binder can be a life-saver. Make lists of all the hotel or venue personnel whom you will be dealing with, names and positions of your volunteers, how each room should be set up, what audio-visual equipment was ordered for each room, food and beverage orders for all sessions, names and phone numbers of your vendors and suppliers, cell phone numbers of the other organizers, and flight numbers and arrival times of your speakers. Do not forget the list of participants! You cannot have enough lists.

You will also want copies of all contracts, permits, insurance papers, shipping and tracking numbers, emergency procedures, contingency plans, and all other important lists, agendas, and timelines. You may want to have a copy of all handouts in case you find yourself making extra copies in the business center five minutes before a session.

NOTE: Have your tool box near at all times as well. You never know when you will need paper clips, Swiss army knife, safety pin, or duct tape in a moment's notice. A suggested list of items to pack is in the following section *Pack a Mobile Office*.

Create Name Badges

One of the most important and noticed items at an event are name badges. The badges provide introduction and promote networking. Make sure they include name, organization, city, and state. You should be able to get this information from the database you created when the participants registered.

Make them readable. Add the logo, use color, and different type sizes, depending on your needs. There are many options for the size and type of paper that can be printed as well as several different holder styles. You can print the badges yourself or have them done professionally.

You might want to use ribbons, different color badges, stars, or decals for the speakers, VIPs, volunteers, or organizers. This is a good way to identify who's who.

Creating Evaluations Forms

Evaluations are a great measuring tool for the success or failure of your event or your speakers. They let you know what parts of your program worked and what needs improvement or deletion. Depending on the scope of your event, you will need one or more evaluation forms.

You can create one to assess the overall event or get more specific and have an evaluation form for each breakout session, speaker, meal, or function. They can be very informative if you are asked to do this event again. You can even ask your participants to rate the facility, the meals, entertainment, staff, and the organization of the event. Items such as the marketing materials or the contact with the hosting company can also be included.

Evaluations can be simple or detailed as you need. If you want a good return of evaluations, keep them short. People tend to be more cooperative if they are short. Allow them to be anonymous but make room for names and other information if they choose to identify themselves.

The more information you can gather, the better the next event will be. You may find that a speaker was not appropriate, the meals were awful, the music was too loud, or the agenda did not make sense. Evaluations can be translated into future profits.

Getting attendees to complete and return their evaluation forms has always been a challenge. To get the best statistical results and a true picture of the event success or failure, you need to get as many forms back as possible. The results will give you the advantage of creating future events that can save you time and money, the ability to attract more attendees, and best of all, save you from future mistakes.

Allow for time to complete evaluation during the event. Do not wait for the very last minute for the guests to complete the assessments. You may want to e-mail a questionnaire within a week or two following the event. You will get a great response. Follow the same rules about short and simple. Be sure not to wait more than two weeks; you want the event to be fresh in their minds.

Provide a deadline for returning and then send a reminder a couple of days before that deadline. Remember that people are very busy.

Make sure the evaluation forms are designed creatively. Stick to one page and ask concise questions. Do a test on the questions with a handful of attendees and colleagues if there is time.

Of course, with today's tech-savvy attendees, sending evaluations electronically via e-mail while they are still at the site or shortly thereafter to their BlackBerrys, Treos, or other handheld devices is a big hit. With data accumulated electronically you can save an incredible amount of time for processing results. You can also have the evaluation on an on-site cyber kiosk.

Sometimes a little encouragement will go along way and will work well to get a better return of your evaluations. Offer a gift or the chance of a gift for those who respond quickly. Have a drawing for something that everyone wants or needs, such as an iPod, or you could enclose an immediate giveaway, something less costly such as a pen or a gift certificate—something useful.

Schedule Volunteers

Prepare a staff assignment list including work schedules, times, and rules (such as no eating at the registration desk). You will need staff for a variety of tasks including working the registration desk, checking meeting rooms for set-up accuracy, taking tickets at meal functions, and checking the audio-visual equipment. Review staff assignments before you go on-site.

Make phone calls, send e-mails or letters, whatever form of communication you decide to use. Make sure all your volunteers understand their duties. What will they be responsible for? What are their shift times? Do they need any more information from you? Having all of this confirmed before the event will save time and avoid confusion.

The Event: Celebrity Waiters Luncheon

Purpose: Fundraiser for high school sports

Participants: Local businesses, sports enthusiasts, media personalities, school administrators

Numbers: 1,000 participants, 75 celebrity waiters, five high school bands, five sets of cheerleaders

This was a fast and furious three-hour event. One thousand meals had to be served by inexperienced sports and celebrity personalities. The entertainment included cheerleaders, bands, and speeches by local school board members and politicians. I was responsible for a number of tasks that day. One task was assigning jobs and directing volunteers. Well, somehow I overlooked a very large and glaring responsibility. The bands! Someone had to meet the buses, direct the band leader and members to a specific spot, tell them what time they were to play, and where to march to and from. There were five bands from five different schools with at least 30 members in each band. I hear through my walkie-talkie that the first band bus has arrived. Where do I direct them? It was at that moment that I realized I did not have anyone down there handling this very important task. What did I do? I quickly went through the list of volunteers I had, what their tasks were, and when their task started. I was able to pull a volunteer off a task that was not as urgent, someone who could handle this task at the last minute and look prepared. Only she and I knew what had happened.

Sharon C., Events Production
Salt Lake City, Utah

Pack Mobile Office

If you are taking your computer, make sure you have all the information and applications saved in case something were to happen to your laptop. Back up all critical PowerPoint presentations or digital photographs. If you are not going to bring your laptop, use a USB memory drive (pen drives, flash drives, and keychain drives). A USB drive for a PC or Mac provides an easy way to download, store, and carry your data. Unlike a CD-ROM, you can erase and load new stuff at will. Have another copy back at the office with someone who can get you a copy of anything you may need.

Pack your portable toolbox with your office supplies and pack your office equipment if needed. Put the following items in your toolbox:

Office supplies: Pack a complete assortment of paper, paper clips, note pads, stapler, staples, transparent tape, masking tape, electrical tape, packing tape, duct tape, walkie talkies, markers, scissors, batteries, tissues, diskettes, rubber bands, glue, receipt book, correction tape, overnight shipping envelopes and boxes, blades for opening boxes, index cards, post-its, calculator, flashlight, pens, pencils, clipboards, tools (such as a screwdriver and hammer), transparencies, pens, aspirin, energy bars, bottled water, loose change and dollar bills, tacks, safety pins, extra name tags, white out, a few extension cords, and a first-aid kit. Add whatever else you might need. When you get all these pertinent items in one or two boxes, label them clearly. These are the boxes you will want to open first upon arrival. Or you may carry it with you if you are traveling by car. Carry a knife or box cutters with you to open your first box. If flying, put it in your luggage. Do not carry it on your person or in your purse. It will be confiscated at the airport.

Office equipment as needed: A computer, printer, copy/fax machine, and associated supplies. The following supplies are cheap insurance, such as a power protector (get one with a built-in phone-line splitter and snap-on clip for tangle-free phone cord storage), a removable flash card for a camera or PD, and a lightweight USB cable, three feet long extended USB cord for various devices and perhaps a hub if several devices will be used at once. For broadband connections for Internet or LAN jack, a portable Ethernet cable cord provides seven feet of cable and will retract into a compact case.

Lists: Keep an on-site meeting equipment and supplies checklist in your event binder. Include:

- All the shipping information.

- Original copies of participant packet materials. (You may need to make copies at the last minute.)

List of names and phone numbers for:

- Organizers, vendors, volunteers with their positions, times, and responsibilities

- Site personnel and their phone numbers

- Speaker's arrival and departure times and phone numbers

- Vendors, names, phone numbers, and arrival information

- Emergency numbers

- Participants' information and payment history

"No self-respecting event planner should go anywhere without a large roll of duct tape."

Jane, real estate associate

Like most event planners, I tend to carry too much when I travel. It is confusing, and my shoulder screams at me that night from the weight of the bag. Of course, the smart thing to do is get the right carry on bag that can hold all of my equipment and accessories in an organized way.

MATERIALS FOR THE EVENT

In meeting situations, conference materials need to be distributed to each participant. If nothing else, there will be name tags, a welcome packet of some kind, and an agenda. There also may be some policies that need to be shared: smoking areas, drinking regulations, and cell phone use.

It may be your policy, or it may be the policy of the site. These policies need to be related to the participants somehow and usually they are inserted with the welcome material upon registration.

Start gathering, printing, and copying the material that will go into the participants' packets. At this point of the planning, you are in the process of collecting speakers' handouts that they will be sharing in their presentation. After all the material is gathered and printed, someone will have to assemble the packets. If the event has 2,000 participants, imagine how long it would take to assemble these packets. This might be a good time to outsource a task. Do not wait until the last minute; there will be plenty of other things to do in the last week!

Remember to take one hard copy of each of the items in your briefcase or carry-on and save another on your computer. If everything else fails, you can take that one handout, agenda, or registration form to a local printing or copy center. Some of the most common materials that go in a packet are:

- Agenda and program

- Alphabetical attendee list (with or without full address info)

- Coupons

- Evaluation forms (overall and specific session)

- Facility map if not included in program

- Giveaways (promotional gifts)

- Invitations to special events

- Last-minute information not in the program

- Letters

- Local maps, brochures, or magazines

- Name badge

- Receipts

- Ribbons

- Special handouts

- Tickets

SHIPPING

When you are ready to pack and ship materials, there are many issues to consider so that you can easily track each item. The better organized you are, the better you can help the shipper find the right (lost) box. More important, you know exactly what is inside the missing box.

First create an organized system for the inventory that goes into the boxes and then organize the boxes themselves. Clearly record what is placed in each box and clearly identify the box on the outside with a numbered system so that you will know exactly what is in box "P1 of 5." For example, use the letter P for your personal items such as your tool box, lists of important documents, and shipping labels. You may want to use a H1 for the presenters' handouts. If you have ten boxes of handouts, your numbering systems would be "H1 of 10," "H2 of 10," and so on.

Create a system that works for you. Label all boxes using the same format. Keep an inventory list of what is in each box, how that box is labeled and what type of box it is, and carry it with you to the destination. Make copies of the list and give them to others on your staff. If a box is missing, you will know exactly which box and what it contains. This may sound like a lot of work but when your carrier tells you that only nine of the ten pieces have arrived, you will know exactly what is missing. You can assist the carrier by saying it is a blue plastic bin with the numbers P5 printed in large red letters on the side.

On the same inventory list, include each tracking number for each box and phone numbers of the carriers. Ask anyone who is shipping items to the meeting site to provide you with the same information.

Make sure you give yourself plenty of time to get boxes shipped. It can get very expensive if you have to rush ship materials that weigh 30 pounds per box. Do not send the boxes too early either as you may be charged a storage fee.

Sometimes your vendors will be shipping materials to your event. Before you leave your office, call your vendors and confirm that they have sent shipments and get all shipping information from them. Get the tracking numbers, shipper's name, address, the date shipped, how many boxes to expect, and the weight.

Also call the site or venue and confirm whether they have received your shipments. The sooner you know that a box is missing, the faster you can find it or replace it. When you are getting confirmation of the piece count, ask the consignee to count the pieces that are in their storage or warehouse rather than read it off a bill of lading. If you do not disclose how many pieces there are supposed to be, there is a higher likelihood that they will actually count the pieces. Looking for missing items on-site is very time consuming, and if important materials are missing it can have a severe impact on the event.

If you are shipping to the hotel before your arrival, ensure that the recipient (consignee) will accept your materials and store them for you. Find out what they will charge for this service. Ask them to check the freight for damages or shortages before they sign the bill of lading. Know whether there are any national holidays in the days and weeks before your event. Holidays can slow the supply chain from warehousing, trucking, and customs. Working hours—particularly with customs— can be different in the country of destination. Know what you are up against when planning your shipment.

Bring preprinted, overnight shipping labels to the event for returning your unused materials and personal items. These are very handy when you need to ship your leftover materials back to the office. Remember to remove any old labels from the boxes before you apply new labels. Old ones have electronic bar codes and can be scanned unintentionally.

Check, Check, and Double Check

I arrived in Minneapolis at the hotel a couple days before our week long intensive was to begin. I always try to arrive early to meet with the venue staff, get the lay of the land and to make sure all our materials arrived. When doing my regular check of the boxes shipped, it turned out that a couple boxes of important handouts did not arrive. Fortunately I had the originals with me and I quickly found the nearest Kinko's and frantically make enough copies. I always travel with a complete set of handouts for this very reason.

A day into this same training, we realized that a few boxes from our video vendor at the California Department of Education (CDE) had yet to arrive. We had them tracked through UPS confirming that the boxes had been delivered to the site. The hotel could not find them. Again we asked the hotel to look for them but to no avail. On our last day there I mentioned that each box of videos was worth around $1,200. That seemed to do the trick and all of a sudden they appeared. Since then we are very consistent in having tracking numbers with us and pressing the hotel to search for boxes until they find them.

Karla Nygaard, Conference Coordinator
Sausalito, CA

Shipping Tips

Each piece should have two shipping labels because labels can be mistakenly turned inward or out of sight or can fall off. When shipments are stacked, your labels may face inside the pallet and be invisible. Two labels are especially helpful when a piece is missing and the warehouse is searching for it. Two labels increase the chances that people will read them.

Using boxes with strong corners decreases the chances of their falling apart in transit. Strengthen the box with packing tape on all the edges and corners. Remember that corners of boxes will crease. Try plastic containers instead of boxes. Corners will not dent and they stack better. Most have handles making them easier to move around.

CHOOSING A CUSTOMS BROKER—FOR OUT OF COUNTRY SHIPPING

When your event is in another country, shipping material becomes challenging. Since each country has unique custom requirements, it is vital to choose a good customs broker, one who is knowledgeable in the country where you will be exporting your goods. Choose a broker who has experience in working with trade shows, conferences, events, and exhibitions. A knowledgeable customs broker can ensure that your goods clear customs and also minimize duties, taxes, and other related fees.

Customs delays of days, or even hours, can mean the difference between having your material at your event or having nothing. Events are scheduled to move in or out after hours and on weekends and even through holidays, requiring your broker to work those same nonstandard hours. Be sure the broker you choose is willing to work on your schedule.

One of the challenges is to understand the rates and charges. Make sure you have in writing what the door-to-door costs will be including any applicable duties and taxes. Understand that you are importing goods to another country and will be dealing with bureaucratic red tape. Allow plenty of time.

The Day Has Arrived!

*L*ights, camera, action! Are you ready? If you followed the timelines and checklists and everything else that has been suggested to you, you should be prepared for action. This section helps you with the finishing touches and tells you what to do when you arrive at the event site. We will walk you through the process from checking into the facility and setting up your office to getting acquainted with the facility staff and setting up your registration area. Also we have tips on what to do while the event is going on. Know this: you will be extremely busy; wear comfortable shoes.

WHAT TO DO WHEN YOU ARRIVE

When the event is large and consuming, try to arrive a day or two before it begins to give yourself time to establish a presence and get comfortable with the surroundings. Have the pre-planning meeting with the sales manager, catering manager, audio-visual department, and the general manager and all other important players when possible. Go over all the details. Make any changes needed during this meeting. Get keys to all the meeting rooms. Introduce the facility members to any members of your team who are authorized to make decisions in case you are unavailable. Let them know who is allowed to order more coffee at the breaks or charge that last-minute order for an extra easel or printing 50 extra handouts.

Establish a chain of command for implementing changes or handling emergencies and communicate it to the facility and to your staff. Review the list of names and cell numbers or extensions and time schedules to know who will be where when. You will want to know if there is a shift change in the middle of your event and if so, when that happens and who is in charge.

Check to see if your equipment, supplies, and materials have arrived. Check them yourself if you can and compare them with your lists. This is important because if there a box is missing, you will have time to hunt it down.

Walk around the site and familiarize yourself with the layout. Get familiar with the hotel staff. Introduce yourself to the front desk personnel. Get to know people by name. Make friends. You will be glad you did.

Set up your office space, unpack, and get organized. Use a separate room dedicated throughout the event. It could be your sleeping quarters or the registration area. Nonetheless, get started setting up your area.

Hang banners and set up signs if the facility will allow. Get directions to the closest copying service, florist, office supply, grocery store, and local caterer. You may need them at a moment's notice. Do as much as you can the day before the event.

If you cannot be at the site before the day of the event, organize yourself enough so that when you do arrive, you can hit the ground running. Make sure that all of your staff is prepared to do the same. If you are meeting the caterers that morning, have your checklist ready to check off equipment and do the same with the tent company, electricians, musicians, and florist. Your agenda should display when the suppliers and vendors are to arrive and what they are responsible for bringing.

Event: All day workshop for 200 Health Professional

Venue: Church auditorium with side room for continental breakfast and registration

This was about the 15th similar workshop held in this city and specific venue. At each workshop we served muffins and coffee during the registration which began at 8:15 a.m. Now these were particular muffins that we ordered and served and they were special enough that we mentioned them in all our marketing materials. They were of the healthy variety and had been a hit among past attendees.

For all other events, the delivery person (same person, same bakery) would come to the venue between 7 and 7:30 a.m. to drop off dozens of boxes and leave. We always made sure there was plenty of time between the delivery and setting up the registration area. This particular morning the delivery person dropped off the boxes without getting a signature because that is how it worked in the past. All the boxes were labeled with the name of the event and the correct address.

One of the volunteers was hungry and decided to have a muffin. As she opened one of the boxes, to her great surprise, there were no muffins but thousands of frozen French fries. Oh no. No one at the meeting had the phone number of the bakery! We quickly gathered, put all of our money together, and sent a couple of the volunteers down to the closest grocery for fruit; fruit that you can eat with your hands.

We needed finger foods because we had plates but no forks. So the morning was saved! The attendees received at least some food as promised. The speaker made note of the story and was able to make light of the situation.

Lesson learned:

Look inside all deliveries.

Have someone specifically assigned to receive and sign for the delivery.

Keep all important phone numbers on hand.

Know your alternate food sources within a five- to ten-minute range of your venue.

Judith Shaw, Coordinator
Bolinas, CA

REHEARSAL

The rehearsal can be done up to a week before the event when possible, though the day before is usually when you get the opportunity because you will be at the site. It will be a dry run of the agenda. It should be done with as many of the staff and volunteers as possible. The rehearsal gives you the opportunity to work out any logistical issues, confirm procedures, and clear up any unanswered questions. Sometimes there will not be time for a rehearsal, but when there is, here are some details you may want to check.

- Is the registration area designed for easy flow of traffic?

- Is the help desk situated in a focal nearby area?

- Do we have all the appropriate supplies and signs?

- Are there stairs leading to the stage that might be a problem for the speakers?

- Is there enough room between tables and chairs for traffic to flow?

- Is the room set up so that everyone can see the stage?

- Have all the signs, lists, and agendas been given to the appropriate people?

The point is, the more organized you are at the rehearsal the more smoothly the event will run.

REGISTRATION CHECK-IN AREA

Registration is where most attendees, exhibitors, vendors, speakers, and even facility staff will go to ask questions and get help. Therefore, it is important to have someone there at all times who can make decisions and answer questions. Remember that your registration staff will be busy. Any questions your staff cannot answer should be referred quickly to someone who can help. If you cannot have the "answer person" remain in the registration area (maybe because it is you and you have to be everywhere), put your staff members on walkie talkies or cell phones to be able to reach you instantly.

If you have hundreds of registrants, ticket holders, or guests (each with an individual registration packet), you may need a large check-in area with registration booths instead of tables and chairs. How you set up registration depends on what kind of materials you are providing. For example, assume all the registration packets contain the same info and the only unique item is the participant's name badge. Here you can place the name badges in alphabetical order on tables. As the participants pick up a name badge, you check off their name and hand them a packet. Done! If the packets are different for each individual, they should be placed in alphabetical order behind registration. If the group is large, break up the registration stations alphabetically, A-F, G-L, M-R, S-Z, for example.

Registration stations and staffing are very critical. Consider the number of participants you will have and break up the registration so that traffic flows easily. Plan for at least one staff person for every 75 participants.

For larger conferences, greeters are a good idea to assist and direct people in getting around the meeting site. Send arriving exhibitors and speakers to different areas and provide them with special assistance geared to their needs.

It is good to have a specific area for money-related issues with a designated troubleshooter who knows all the ropes and can solve any problem or issue that will arise.

Remember that the majority of guests will arrive about the same time. Be prepared for them to get what they need and move on. Even if they are coming to a party without a necessary check-in point, keeping them from clogging the entry way is crucial. Do not have the bar or appetizers right inside the entry door. Move the people toward the back of the room when possible.

Signs

Use signs to give your participants directions. Direct them to the bathrooms, tell them where to register, direct them anywhere that something pertaining to the event is happening. Let them know where to find the book sellers, exhibits, excursion sign-up, transportation information, lost and found, rest rooms, and phones.

Give them as much directional information as possible. Do not make them ask. The easier it is for the participant to move around the event, the better the traffic flow will be, and less information will be asked of you and your staff.

Be as clear as possible with your signs. Make your signs at least eight feet off the floor for visibility. Be sure that your signs are appropriate for the event.

ON-SITE MANAGEMENT

Magic can occur if you are well organized. Remember, plan for the best outcome but be prepared for the unexpected and remain calm.

Staff and Volunteers

Volunteers and staff may be the first encounter for your participant. Whatever you do, keep your staff and volunteers happy.

Make sure you have enough volunteers and they are prepared to greet the participants. Arm them with enough information to answer all questions or to point them to someone who can. Make sure they have all the materials needed to register the participants and be of assistance.

You may want one person to be responsible for all the volunteers. This person not only shows them what they need to do, but she can bring them water and snacks too. Train your staff:

- To wear an attitude that is truly welcoming to everyone.

- Be prepared to solve problems.

- Be comfortable and professional.

- Be willing to replace another position in case of emergency or bathroom break.

- Smile at all times.

Another handy thing to have is a list of frequently asked questions by attendees. Brainstorm with staff and key volunteers in advance to identify the questions you think attendees will ask your registration desk personnel and list the answers. Here are some typical questions:

- Where are the bathrooms?

- How can I pay for the event?

- Can I pay by check or credit card? Which ones do you accept? Where is the nearest bank or ATM?

- Where are the meeting rooms? Have your staff become familiar with the floor plan.

- I need to cancel the last day. Can I get a refund?

- I have a special meal request. Whom do I tell?

- Is Suzie Q. registered for the conference? Has she checked in yet? Can I leave a message for her?

- Where can I get breakfast, lunch, or dinner?

Also it is essential that you train your staff on the emergency procedures of the hotel. They should know what to do in the event of any crisis. Make sure you know the facility's emergency procedures and communicate them to your entire staff.

Inspect the Meeting Rooms

Have someone inspect each meeting room at least 30 minutes before a session begins. See that the room set-up is correct and the audio-visual equipment is there and working! There is nothing worse than having a speaker begin talking into a microphone that is not working or emits a loud squeal.

Know where the lights and thermostats are in every room. Rooms should be cool in the morning because after people arrive, the room will warm up. Do not rush in turning up the heat; hot rooms create sleepy participants.

Do not depend on the hotel staff to prepare the rooms fully. Check each room yourself or have volunteers for the job. Just check them out! Inspect the rooms after the meeting is over. Participants may have left belongings behind.

Do the same for your refreshment breaks. Make sure they are set up on time and there is the correct amount of each item you ordered. Is the coffee hot enough? Were there enough cookies? You would be surprised how this simple order can go wrong. You do not want your sessions to break when the refreshment station is not completely set up or to have the food or beverage run out before all participants have had the chance to indulge.

This also applies to any food and beverage function such as receptions, buffet dining, and mid-morning and mid-afternoon breaks.

At the End of the Day

Get the master bill from the facility and review it while everything is still fresh in your mind. Go over all charges. Make changes immediately if needed. If your event is longer than one day, doing a review every day will save you from having to remember what went on two or three days ago. Mark up the statement and speak with someone right away. You can also go over the number of items that you were short or ran out of early and adjust the numbers for the next day. Before you retire, review tomorrow's function sheets with the appropriate site managers.

CONTINGENCY PLAN

No event, no matter how well planned and well run, is immune from an occasional calamity or crisis. Problems can arise in any area, at any time, anywhere, and as planners, we need to be prepared. They can be small such as boxes not arriving on time to full-blown disasters such as fires, hurricanes, and earthquakes. Even the threat of terrorism or other health-related scares can change dramatically in a moment's notice. You cannot possibly plan for all situations, but a good event planner must have a contingency plan and an emergency plan in place. Your event site should already have an existing plan; ask to have a copy and spend some time going over it with your staff and volunteers. Better safe than sorry.

There is the plan for the day of the event emergency and then there is a big picture contingency plan for the large-scale, totally uncontrollable occurrence such as natural disasters, political unrest in a particular area of the globe, or even health scares that can change things weeks or months before the event. Plan for the unexpected always.

If your event is outside, do you have a contingency plan for bad weather? What will you do with 500 people when it is raining in the middle of July and the picnic grounds you have rented has hundreds of puddles?

What do you do when you get a phone call from your keynote speaker the day before the event saying she has laryngitis? What will you do when the caterer is two hours late for a sit down reception for 200? What happens to your event when there is a major traffic jam and half your participants will not arrive on time or at all?

I went to El Salvador for a conference that was scheduled during the broadcast of the World Cup. I was given a time to speak because my company was the marquis sponsor. Unfortunately, at the exact same time I was scheduled to start my session, Japan was playing Brazil and, not surprisingly, no one showed up for my session. The event planners were red-faced and apologetic, and I was slightly embarrassed. They ended up rescheduling my session for the next day but I only had 15 minutes to speak during breakfast. Not everyone showed up and I was only able to present a quarter of my material. The moral of this story is make sure you understand the priorities of a foreign culture before you create your agenda. Plan for last-minute changes due to uncontrollable circumstances.

Ingrid

Part of being an event planner is the ability to think on your feet and come up with alternatives and quick fixes. Always be prepared!

- Develop an emergency plan before arriving on-site. When the event is large, take time to put your plans into writing, increasing the chances that everyone will follow it in the event of a crisis.

- Review your insurance coverage before your event. It is likely that your insurance needs may be different from year to year depending on the venue you are using and the types of activities included in your meeting.

- Hire emergency medical technicians to work on-site at your event. Make sure they will be available throughout the event and that all staff members know how to reach them.

- Communicate safety information to attendees. Consider providing safety tips and emergency procedures in individual registration packets.

- Stock your staff office with emergency gear. Some important items to keep on hand include a first aid kit, a weather radio, and an attendee list with their emergency contacts. Some planners even print emergency contact information on the backs of attendee name badges.

Planners need to be ready for different challenges today such as new technology, changing personnel, changing demographics of your participants, economic downturns or upswings, labor issues, needs and wants of the public, our services and products, as well as the increasing globalization of just about everything. Although these may not be considered emergencies, they are issues that you must take into consideration and be prepared for. If you have spent a great deal of money setting up an event in Hawaii for a week-long conference and the economy takes a turn for the worse in your industry, what are your backup plans? What if the airline mechanics go on strike that week or your largest group of participants just got laid off because the company CEO was caught embezzling? These scenarios do happen.

Event: Holiday Party
Company Employees and guests: 350

Two days before a large company holiday party at an elegant, private mansion in the Buckhead area of Atlanta, the home burned to the ground. In less than one day I had to find another location and alert everyone involved.

Because I had so many contacts in Atlanta, I started calling, begging for assistance. It was the holidays in the City and if you do not book a venue early, you are either out of luck or you will get the bottom of the barrel for choices.

Tenacity prevailed and a mansion not far from the original spot was found, but that meant getting new decorations, re-arranging parking, and revisiting site plans. They now would need valets because the new site had no public parking. Buses had to be rented and positioned at the old site to transport guests back and forth to new site.

Because I was quick on the draw and had hundreds of contacts in the City, I was able to pull off the party hardly disturbing the flow of the event and the participants. It was fortunate that the company had money to pick up the extra costs and wanted to have the show go on.

Linda D., Event Planner
Atlanta, Georgia

After the
Show

The last participant has departed, the volunteers and staff are gone, and the show is over! Take a deep breath and congratulate yourself. If you remained calm and serene with a smile on your face, no one knows what actually went on behind the scenes. The participants probably did not even notice all the last-minute changes, substitutions, or near mistakes.

Tying up loose ends like paying bills and generating reports is the final task of your event. Pre-arrange a debriefing meeting with everyone involved to review the event within the following week so that it is still fresh in everyone's mind. Be sure to make an extensive thank-you list and begin the appreciation process. Follow up on the evaluation forms you requested from your participants and start tracking your event. All of this information will be incredibly valuable for your next event. Do not reinvent the wheel or make the same mistakes next time. No event will be exactly the same but the information will be priceless.

Was your vision realized? Did the event make money, lose money, or just break even? Did you achieve your return on investment goals, your financial goals? What did you like or not like about each aspect of the event? The questions and answers will guide you to keep certain characteristics and discard others.

PAY THE BILLS

To alleviate problems with the final bills, it is recommended that if your event is longer than one day, you review all charges at the end of each day. When it comes to the end of the event, you will be ahead of the master bill reviewing process. In some cases, your master bill will come well after the meeting is over. Keep all daily accounts of your charges and go over your contract to make sure both you and the vendor have met your obligations. Also look for last-minute additions to your bill such as shipping, food and beverage, or audio-visual charges. More than likely if your event was big, there will be an error on the master bill. Always double check!

Get copies of the final report from the facility including how many rooms were booked, all the numbers of food and beverages, and audio-visual usage. If possible, find out how participants used the facilities such as restaurants, pools and spas, and room service. This information will be helpful if you repeat the event next month or next year.

DEBRIEFING MEETING

Everyone who participated in the decisions and planning of the event should attend the debriefing meeting if possible. This is an opportunity to go over the things that went right and those things that need improvement. Please do not use this meeting to do any blaming. What is done is done. Move on and take appropriate steps to ensure that it does not happen next time. Come up with additional questions specific to your event. Some questions you might cover:

- What worked; what did not?

- What would we do differently next time?

- Were your goals and objectives met?

- Did you realize your defined vision?

- Did you come in on budget? Did you spend more in one area than anticipated? Why?

- What unanticipated expenditures did we have? Were they necessary?

- Did your participants seem to enjoy certain aspects over others?

- Were the speakers or entertainment appropriate?

- Was the food appropriate?

- Were the lighting, staging, and sound right?

THANK YOUS

Say "thank you" to everyone and do it soon after the event. Be specific! When appropriate, put your thank-yous in the form of a letter, although, in some cases, a phone call will suffice. Some very helpful people are warranted a gift of some kind. It does not have to be expensive, just thoughtful. Do not hold back in the area of appreciation. Especially thank all of your volunteers. Many people worked very hard to make your event successful. Make sure they know how much they meant to that success. Do not forget your vendors; they also need to know that their services and personnel did a good job. Remember, you will need them next time!

FOLLOW-UP EVALUATIONS

Tabulate the evaluations right away before you are on to your next project. They provide important information that you can use for your future events. Prepare an organized summation to include some of your personal interpretations and recommendations. Disperse the summation to all the decision makers and planners that were involved.

If you had separate evaluations for each speaker, provide them with a copy of their evaluations and keep a copy for your records.

FINAL REPORT

Put everything in a final event report. This just means consolidating all the information into one place. The information is used to track your history. Use this report for future events.

Put at least the following information in your report:

- Event name, dates, and location

- Goals and objectives—defined vision

- Number of participants—paid

- Number of participants—complimentary (VIP's, sponsors, staff, and cancellations)

- The facility report with the number of rooms, food, and beverage

- Evaluation summation

- Any conclusions you made from the debriefing meeting

- Copies of all marketing material

- Copies of all handouts and agendas

- Your timelines and checklists

- Budget estimate

- List of all volunteers and staff

- Record your suppliers; include phone number, key information, and any evaluation you have of them. You may want to use them again

- Evaluations

- Copies of all invoices

Now go get a massage!

Appendix

Event Planning Industry

Many people come into the meeting and event industry by accident or by reasons other than by choice. So how does one become a great event planner from the beginning?

The event planning industry is growing. It is a vibrant, exciting, yet young industry. In the United States there are about 325,000 professional event planners. These numbers are growing as the industry is becoming a recognizable profession. In the last 25 years, meeting and event planning has created associations and affiliations with its own set of standards, procedures, and certifications, making the profession viable and ethical. The meeting industry has a multitude of organizations and affiliations that offer products and services to planners. There is a list of Internet Web sites listing dozens of these organizations and more in the References section.

The industry is growing because the business world is holding more meetings and events. There will always be events that need an experience and dedicated planner.

ASSOCIATIONS AND ORGANIZATIONS

Planning associations, organizations, and affiliations are dedicated to providing continuing education, conferences, and seminars on the latest trends, books and newsletters, and are valuable place for networking, plus they offer many other important services.

Becoming a member of one of these organizations is not required to be a meeting planner, but it is important that you know that they exist and what they have to offer.

Note: We are not recommending any of these organizations in particular; we are just informing you of their existence.

The most respected associations today are:

- Meeting Professionals International (MPI)

- Certified Meeting Planners (CMP)

- Professional Convention Management Association (PCMA)

- American Society of Association Executives (ASAE)

There are associations tailored to specific market segments such as corporate, association, government, and special events. Some are on the international, national, state, or local levels. Before you join make sure that these associations have value for you and your specific field of planning. Membership fees can be expensive.

Some of the value they offer you:

- Networking

- Continuing Education

- Events

- Certification

- Reference Access

- Credibility

- Employment Opportunities

- Contacts Around the World

Networking is high on the list of values. Having availability to people and places in the industry is golden. You never know when you will need a resource at a moment's notice. If event planning is your career path, be active whenever you can, get involved, and be a resource for others.

TRADE PUBLICATIONS

Publications offer another great tool for keeping up with the industry trends. These magazines often contain articles on job opportunities, destination options, salary information, hotel and resort data, industry best practices, meeting and planning strategies, contracting and legal information, and who's who in the business.

Some associations have trade publications as a part of their membership. See the Reference section for a partial list.

QUALITIES OF AN EVENT PLANNER

The role of event coordinator is a demanding one. Your responsibilities change from day to day and from minute to minute. You must be able to remember details, manage personnel, plan your budget, administer and coordinate multiple activities, have some marketing knowledge and good administration skills. A few necessary traits of a great planner are:

- **Organizational skills and an eye for detail** — An event planner should be detail-oriented with the ability to make a comprehensive plan of attack, someone with good time management skills, the ability to keep an activity log, create and follow timelines, concentrate on results, do what is important, set daily goals, and make priority lists.

- **The ability to develop and maintain interpersonal relationships** — The ability to build good relationships is critical. These relationships may include your clients, staff, servers, balloon company, director of operations, and the CEO of a fortune 500 company. Having the ability to communicate with each of these diverse types will make for strong relationships.

- **Have great written and oral communication skills** — You must be articulate and professional. Verbal communication and good writing skills are necessary. The ability to read non-verbal signals and the ability to listen and pay attention are very useful and important skills. Also it is important to be willing and confident enough to ask questions.

- **Be creative** — A creative person can offer the unexpected and be unique, can brainstorm with others involved, discuss all ideas, pay attention to the latest fads and keep informed of trends of the trade.

- **Levelheaded and a quick thinker** — Having the ability to work under pressure goes along way in this business. No matter how organized you are, something will unexpectedly come up and it will be your job to solve the problem quickly and quietly. It is the nature of the business. You need to have the skill to remain calm and think on your feet.

- **Determination and Persistence** — Never settle for the status quo. Be persistent with people who can get you what you need, permits, for example. Do not be afraid to call in the big guns when needed.

- **Good negotiation skills** — Negotiation is very important for both you and your client. You need to be able to negotiate your fee and vendors' prices. Making it a win-win situation for everyone involved is the key. Knowing the right person to negotiate with is crucial as well as having the appropriate knowledge of what the right prices are in that industry. If they will not negotiate with money, there may be other things worth negotiating for such as extra rooms, free parking, or an additional meeting room for your office at a conference. Just remember to ask for what you want!

NEGOTIATIONS SKILLS AND STRATEGIES

"In business, you do not get what you deserve; you get what you negotiate."

Chester Karrass, Founder of Effective Negotiating™

Knowing how to get what you want is a key attribute for an event planner. Negotiating is an acquired skill that can be polished with experience.

A good negotiator has the ability to get more money, get more of what they want, have productive relationships, head off misunderstandings, and settle conflicts that may arise. A planner does all this in a professional and effective way with all types of people.

Negotiating is an integral part of our daily lives even if we are not aware of it. It is important to negotiate well. A good negotiator can get to the point quickly and astutely saving time and money. Here are few strategies to hone your negotiation skills:

- Look at both sides of the deal when asking for changes. Make sure that the end result has benefits for both parties. It is an exchange of value.

- Negotiate in stages. Do not ask for everything right up front. It is definitely a process.

- Know what you want, where you can compromise, what

you can give up, and have alternatives when making the deal.

- Know what the alternative is before you begin negotiating.

- Seek to understand the other side's position by knowing what they want, knowing what is important to them, and knowing what options the other side possesses.

- Come to the table fully armed with as much information as possible.

- Give enough information to the other party that they can make appropriate decisions.

- Find a favorable middle ground.

- Do not be emotional about the outcome.

- Ask for it all and look good when you can compromise by letting a few things go.

- Do not accept the first offer. Make a counter offer.

- Negotiate with the appropriate decision maker from the beginning.

- Be open to splitting the difference instead of accepting a solid no.

- Leave the sticky issues till last. Focus on the easier issues first.

ETHICS

Planners often make decisions with large financial implications. Vendors try to get your business and use many ways to do so. It can be through kickbacks, tickets to the opera, or box seats at the football game. Where do you draw the line when accepting gifts offered by vendors, clients, and suppliers? When confronted with the choice of taking an incentive, bribe, or gift from a supplier consider the consequences of your actions. Can it affect your reputation if everyone knew about it; is it reasonable and fair, or is it extravagant? Is it in violation of someone's trust? What is the intention and spirit in which it is given? Is it inappropriate, unfair, and only for personal gain? How do you feel about it? If you have any negative feeling about it, do not do it; it is not right for you.

Familiarization ("fam") trips can be multi-day trips that are typically all-expense paid to inspect properties and destination cities. This is very common offer to planners to get familiar with what a site or city has to offer. The question you need to ask yourself is: are you seriously considering this city and venue? If not, then your intentions may be unethical.

Kickbacks or rebates are also common in several businesses in the event industry. Hotels may give rebates on sleeping room counts, transportation companies may offer a 10 percent kick back on total sales, or a travel agent may give a free tickets as incentives. These are common but how far should you go with them?

It is not black and white; the lines can be blurred. It is how you feel at the end of the day; did everyone get the best deal? Did you compromise yourself in any way? Is it a win-win for all? Is this something you have to hide or can you share it with others without guilt? These questions and more should be considered before you say yes to an offer that may be unethical.

Early in my career I was responsible for the logistics of a very large multi-day conference. One of my responsibilities was to find bus transportation for 800 people from eight different hotels traveling round trip each day. As I was obtaining bids, one bus company offered me, as the coordinator, a 10 percent bonus fee. Wow. That was a substantial amount of money, especially since I was on a small hourly wage. After wrestling with my intention, I took the situation to my clients and asked what they thought. It would have been so easy to take the money, but my conscience bothered me. They ultimately said pick the best company for the job and if you receive a bonus, take it. So, indeed I found the best company for the job and received a bonus. I slept well at night.

Cindy M.
San Rafael, CA

EMPLOYERS THAT HIRE EVENT PLANNERS

There are dozens of businesses that are in need of event and meeting planning specialists. The job opportunities are endless. Here is a partial list:

Event Planning Companies

- **Incentive Houses** – They specialize in developing programs to motivate employees.

- **Destination Management Companies** – They provide local event planning services for companies that want to hold an event in a different city. They handle all the on-site details for the group. They are hired for their local knowledge and resources to plan tours, meetings, and conventions.

- **Event Planning Firms** – You can find local event planning company listings in the phone directory, your chamber of commerce, or through the Internet.

- **Public Relations Firms** — Ask if event planning is part of their service because not all PR firms handle such events.

- **Advertising Agencies** — Similar to PR firms, not all advertising agencies handle event planning. Some agencies that are full service will do some event planning.

Hospitality Industry

The hospitality industry offers many job opportunities in the event industry. Jobs in the hospitality industry usually provide services to event planners. There are a variety of jobs in this industry and may include a combination of services.

- **Hotels and Resorts** — Hotels and resorts host numerous events: banquets, business meetings, and weddings. Sales and caterings, sales and marketing, or sales manager positions offer experience in event planning. Whether it is booking rooms or helping to select menus for a party, there is valuable experience in hotels and resorts. All major hotel chains have Web sites.

- **Tourism Organizations** — Convention and Visitor Bureaus (CVB) act as a community's official destination management company and offer dozens of services. They are a resource for the event planner. Working for a CVB will get you unlimited contacts and experience in the event planning arena.

- **Clubs** — These types of destinations can be a great place to work. Some clubs have in-house event planners while others hire outside consultants. Clubs host numerous types of events. Some clubs where you can get event planning experience are country clubs, cultural centers, golf clubs, military clubs, private clubs, university faculty clubs, or yacht clubs.

- **Cruise Lines** — Many staff members work on dry land but there are jobs that actually are onboard. It is another great resource for getting event planning experience.

- **Vendors** — Vendors and suppliers offer a variety of job opportunities. These positions will give you the chance to assist clients in planning events. Some of these include caterers and party rental companies.

- **Attractions** — Any place that attracts tourists will offer event planning opportunities. Many hold events to promote themselves or rent out their facility for events.

Some attractions are amusement parks, aquariums, casinos, family fun centers, factory tours, ghost towns, historic sites, monuments, museums, national and state parks, performing arts, professional sports teams, raceways, scenic trains, theme parks, visitor centers, wineries, and zoos.

The Corporate Market

The corporate market includes corporations, associations, non-profit organizations, educational institutions, governmental offices, and hospitals. You can work for one of these businesses as a meeting planner, in administration, in corporate communications, human resources, marketing, member relations, or public relations.

- **Corporations** — Most large corporations have in-house event departments and staff. In smaller companies events usually fall to the office manager or someone in human resources. Occasionally they may hire out.

- **Trade and Professional Associations** — This market offers tremendous opportunities for event planners. These are many groups with a common interest that hold annual conventions and a variety of other events.

- **Non-Profits** — This is another incredible market for event planners. Non-profits are continuously holding fundraisers and other special events.

- **Government** — There is an incredible market for event planners in government. All types of events are planned by cities, states, and individual departments. Keep in mind the political arena and all the events produced around election time.

- **Educational Facilities** — Schools are another great market for event planners. Consider homecoming events, fundraisers, alumni activities, ground breaking festivities, conferences, seminars, and symposiums.

Resources

There are thousands of companies, corporations, associations, and industries that supply information to assist you in performing your job. Listed here are names and Web page addresses for your convenience. You can surf the Internet and find many more.

At the print date of this book, all Web addresses were working. Some may already be out of date by the time you log on. We apologize if that happens. Know that just because they are listed here, we do not personally recommend or endorse a product, service, vendor, or organization. This is just a service to you. Go ahead and search for others. They are out there! And do your own due diligence if you choose to work with any of these resources.

ASSOCIATIONS AND ORGANIZATIONS	
www.ahiattorneys.org	Academy of Hospitality Industry Attorneys
www.ahma.com	American Hotel and Motel Association
www.amanet.org	American Management Association

ASSOCIATIONS AND ORGANIZATIONS	
www.ammc.org	Alliance of Meeting Management Consultants
www.asaenet.org	American Society of Association Executives
www.ascap.com	American Society of Composers, Authors, and Publishers
www.astd.org	American Society of Training & Development
www.astnet.com	American Society of Travel Agents
www.asae.com	American Society of Association Executives
www.acced-i.edu	Assoc. of Collegiate Conferences and Events Directors – Int'l
www.acte.org	Assoc. of Corporate Travel Executives
www.nsfre.org	Assoc. of Fundraising Professionals
www.bbb.com	Better Business Bureau
www.bmi.com	Broadcast Music, Inc.
www.cemadine.com	Computer Event Marketing Associates
www.conventionindustry.org	Convention Industry Council
www.esta.org	Entertainment Services and Technology Associations
www.hsmai.org	Hotel Sales and Marketing Association International
www.iacconline.org	International Association of Conference Centers
www.iacvb.org	International Association of Convention and Visitors Bureaus
www.iaem.org	International Association for Exhibition

ASSOCIATIONS AND ORGANIZATIONS	
www.iasbweb.org	International Association of Speakers Bureaus
www.ifea.com	International Festivals and Events Association
www.iami.org	International Society of Meeting Planners
www.ises.com	International Special Events Society
www.mpiweb.org	Meeting Professionals International
www.nsaspeaker.org	National Speakers Association
www.ncbmp.com	National Coalition of Black Meeting Planners
www.officialtravelinfo.com	Official Travel Guide.com
www.pcma.org	Professional Convention Management Association
www.sesac.com	Performing Rights Organization for Songwriters and Publishers
www.scmp.org	Society of Corporate Meeting Planners
www.sgmp.org	Society of Government Meeting Professionals

INDUSTRY JOBS	
www.coachfederation.org	International Coach Federation
www.hcareers.com	Hospitality Careers Online
www.hotel-jobs.com	Hospitality Jobs Online
www.meetingjobs.com	Meeting Candidate Network
www.mim.com	Meetings Industry Job Board
www.nace.net	Catering Professionals
www.searchwide.com	Search Wide Hospitality Recruitment Experts

CERTIFICATIONS AND ACCREDITATIONS	
www.asaenet.org	Certified Association Executive (CAE)
www.conventionindustry.org	Certified Meeting Professional (CMP)
www.hsmai.org	Certified Hospitality Marketing Executive (CHME)
www.iaam.org	Certified Facilities Executive (CFE)
www.ises.com	Certified Special Events Professional (CSEP)
www.mpiweb.org	Certification in Meeting Management (CMM)
www.nace.net	Certified Professional Catering Executive (CPCE)
www.nsaspeaker.org	Certified Speaking Professional (CSP)
www.site-intl.org	Certified Incentive and Travel Executive (CITE)

MEETING AND EVENT MANAGEMENT RESOURCES	
www.enterprising-events.com	Enterprising Events (coaching, consulting, training)
www.all-hotels.com	All-Hotels.com
www.chamberofcommerce.com	Certified Hospitality Marketing Executive (CHME)
www.conferencedirect.com	Conference Direct
www.conferon.com	Conferon
www.expoexchange.com	Meeting Registration – full service
www.findspeakersandbureaus.com	Speaker Bureaus by State or Country
www.gale.com	Gale Research, Inc.
www.eventsecurity.com	Event Security resources

MEETING AND EVENT MANAGEMENT RESOURCES	
www.eventweb.com	EventWeb
www.helmsbriscoe.com HelmsBriscoe	HotRatesHotDates
www.meetingscoach.com	MeetingsCoach
www.meetingsitesre-sources.net	Meeting Sites Resources
www.meetingsnet.com	Meeting Planners Survival Guide
www.mim.com	Meetings Industry Mall
www.mpoint.com	Plansoft
www.officequest.com	OfficeQuest
www.officespace.com	OfficeSpace
www.officialtravelguide.com	Official Travel Guide
www.pmpn.com	Professional Meeting Planners Network
www.shindigz.com	Shindigz (Special theme kits)
www.speaker.com	Speakers Platform
www.speakersbureaus.org	Speakers Bureau
www.seatguru.com	Airline Seating
www.tia.org	Travel Industry Association
www.worldspeakerasso-ciation.org	World Speakers Association
www.reedtravelgroup.com	REED Travel Group
www.tradeshowresearch.com	Successful Exhibiting
www.uniquevenues.com	Guide to Unique Meeting & Event Facilities
www.zagat.com	Hotel, Restaurant, venue reviews

MEETING TECHNOLOGY SOFTWARE	
www.123signup.com	123 Sign Up
www.bluedot.com	BlueDot.com
www.b-there.com	B-There.com
www.cardscan.com	CardScan
www.cvent.com	Cvent.com
www.dea.com	Event Management Systems
www.certain.com	Event Planner Plus & Meeting Planner Plus
www.ekeba.com	Complete Event Manager
www.eventsource.com	EventSource.com
www.eventregistration.com	Event Registration
www.event411.com	Event411.com
www.evite.com	Online invitations
www.expocad.com	Expocad
www.wififreespot.com/hotels.html	Hotel directory for free wireless
www.meetingmatrix.com	MeetingMatrix
www.mpoint.com	Plansoft
www.netsimplicity.com	Meeting Room Manager
www.optimumsettings.com	Optimum Settings
www.passkey.com	Passkey.com
www.pcnametag.com	PCnametag.com
PeoplewarePro	PeoplewarePro
www.psitrak.com	MeetingTrak
www.regweb.com	RegWeb
www.seeuthere.com	seeUthere.com
www.starcite.com	StarCite

MEETING TECHNOLOGY SOFTWARE	
www.timesaversoftware.com	Room Viewer & Event Sketch
www.viewcentral.com	ViewCentral

WEBCONFERENCING	
www.gotomeeting.com	Online Meetings
www.on24.com	Webcast Provider
www.intercall.com	Global Conferencing solutions
www.convenos.com	Virtual Meeting Space
www.readytalk.com	Audio and Web Conferencing
www.cjfconferencing.com	Audio, Web and Video Conferencing

TRADE PUBLICATIONS	
www.btnonline.com	Business Travel News
www.bizbash.com	Biz Bash online
www.meetings-conventions.com	Meetings and Conventions
www.meetingnet.com	Corporate Meetings and Incentive
www.mimegasite.com	Meeting Industry Megasites
www.midwestmeetings.com	Midwest Meetings
www.meetings411.com	Meetings Focus
www.promomagazine.com	www.promomagazine.com
www.smallmarketmeetings.com	Small Market Meetings
www.smartmtgs.com	Smart Meetings
www.specialevents.com	Special Events
www.successmtgs.com	Successful Meetings

TRADE PUBLICATIONS	
www.wheremagazine.com	Where Magazine

MESSAGE BOARDS-VIRTUAL COMMUNITIES-BLOGS	
www.eventplanning.meetup.com	Event Planning Meet Up
www.mmaweb.com/meetings/meetingboard/	www.groups.yahoo.com/search?query=event+planning
www.groups.yahoo.com/search?query=event+planning	Yahoo!Groups: Event Planning
www.Jobs.associationtrends.com	Job Trends
www.nwmeetings.com/messageboard/topics_long.xml	Northwest Meetings
www.meetingscommunity.org	Online Community for Event Planners
http://groups.google.com/group/MiForum	Online forum of meeting planners
www.meetingsnet.com/blogs/	Meetings Net

ENVIRONMENTAL RESOURCES	
www.bluegreenmeetings.org/	Resource for hosts and planners
www.carbonfund.org	Supports renewable energy, efficiency, and reforestation projects

ENVIRONMENTAL RESOURCES	
www.ceres.org/our_work.htm	Coalition for Environmentally Responsible Economies – Green Hotel Initiative Investors and Environmentalist
www.cleanerandgreener.org/eventcertification/certifiedevents.htm	Event Certification for Cleaner and Greener events
www.climateneutralnetwork.org/	Net zero impact suggestions
www.clintonglobalinitiative.org	Clinton Global Initiative – inspiring change
www.dinegreen.com/	Green Restaurant Association
www.ecobusinesslinks.com	Environmental Directory
www.ecocycle.org	Building a Zero Based Community
www.economicallysound.com/	ECOnomically Sound resources for hospitality services
www.ecotourism.org	International Ecotourism Society
http://epa.gov/greenpower/partners/	List of businesses who support power sources that improve the environment
www.greenmeetings.info/	Green Meeting Industry Council
www.grrn.org/zerowaste	Grassroots Recycling Network
www.greenhotels.com	List of Green Hotels
www.greenfieldpaper.com	Tree Free and Handmade Paper
http://greenseal.org/certification/standards/lodgingproperties.cfm	Green Seals' Standard for Lodging Properties
www.livingtreepaper.com	Tree Free and Recycled Paper
www.meetingstrategiesworldwide.com	Making a difference one event at a time

ENVIRONMENTAL RESOURCES	
www.nativeenergy.com	Carbon Offsetting
www.newleafpaper.com	Environmentally responsible and economically sound paper products
www.pacificforest.org/services/climate.html	Forest Carbon Credits
www.zerowaste.com	Sound Resource Management
www.zerowasteamerica.org	Environmental Resource Organization

Checklists

Event Task Status Report

Event Location:			Date of Event:		
Type of Event:			Coordinator:		
Beginning Date of Report:			End Date of Report:		
Activity	**Start Date**	**Complete Date**	**Person Responsible**	**Notes**	**Status**
Agenda					
Faculty/Speaker/ Entertainment selection					
Destination Selection					
Site Selection					
Budget					
Travel/ Transportation					
Design and Printing					
Marketing					
Environmental Standards					
Audio Visual					
Food and Beverage					
Room assignments and setup					
Event Materials					
Advertising					
Web Design					
Registration Forms					
Ticket Sales					
Publicity					

Event Location:			Date of Event:		
Type of Event:			Coordinator:		
Beginning Date of Report:			End Date of Report:		
Activity	Start Date	Complete Date	Person Respon- sible	Notes	Status
Contacts					
Security					
Sleeping Rooms					
Staffing					
Gifts					
Photographer					
Rentals					
Signs					
Technology Needs					
Hiring Outside Help					
Decorations					
Committees					

Defining Your Event

Tasks	Notes	Due Date
Have pre-planning meeting		
Confirm defined vision		
Identify your goals and objectives		
Confirm financial goals		
Create environmental standards		
Define roles and responsibilities		
Begin Talking about the Budget		
Begin to develop timelines and checklists		
Decide what information will be shared?		
What are the target dates?		
Develop agenda, format, outline		
Define type of site required		
Research site locations		
Define type of event to have		
Identify participants and their demographics		
Decide how to get message out		
Break down tasks assignments		
Create committees		
Begin talking about promotional materials		
How will we get our massage out?		
Determine how to set your fee?		
Will outside vendors be hired?		
Decide if outside coordination help is needed		
Who will be our speakers/ entertainers?		
Create request for proposal		

Budgeting

Here is a list of expenses to get you started. Some will be appropriate for your event and some expenses are not included here. Create your own list to suit your event.

Activity/Items	Estimate Cost	Actual Costs
Accommodations		
Activities – extracurricular		
Administrative overhead		
Advertising		
Audio/Visual equipment		
Awards		
Bartenders		
Communications – cell phones, pagers, radios, copiers, computer		
Entertainment		
Food and Beverage		
Freight and Shipping		
Furniture/electronic rentals		
Gifts for speakers, VIPs, volunteers		
Insurance		
Labor Charges		
Legal Services		
Lodging for speakers/VIPs		
Meeting Planner		
Personnel / Staffing		
Photographer / Photography		
Postage / Mailing		
Promotional Materials/Printing		
Public relations		
Registration Materials		

Activity/Items	Estimate Cost	Actual Costs
Registration service/Ticket service		
Security		
Set-up and take down		
Signs/Decorations		
Speakers / Faculty / Entertainers		
Staging and Lighting and Special Effects		
Supplies		
Tables and Chairs		
Taxes		
Technicians		
Transportation		
Travel for speakers/VIPs		
Venue – location		
Web site design		

Site Selection

Tasks	Notes
Create request for proposal and send them out	
Obtained several bids from several sites.	
Arranged site visits with sites that meet your criteria	
Does venue have adequate space for both meeting and sleeping?	
Is there available function space?	
Do they meet your environmental standards?	
What kind of food and beverage services on-site?	
Do they have audio visual services and technicians on-site?	
Is the venue close to other attractions?	
Is there ample parking?	
Are the rates within our budget?	
Do they have comfortable sleeping rooms?	
Are they close to airport?	
Do they have a pool, spa, weight room?	
What kind of transportation is availability?	
Are they recommended by the CVB?	
Get a copy of menus and f/b services?	
Are there any renovation going on during our dates?	
Are there hotels close by for overflow?	
Are there adequate flights available to city?	
Restaurants on-site or in the vicinity?	
Is their shuttle from/to airport free?	
Is there a Concierge?	
Are they ADA compliant?	
Do they have room service?	
Is the venue in a safe neighborhood?	

Speakers Arrangements

Once you have a verbal agreement with a faculty member or speaker or presenter paperwork needs to exchange hands. You could create a checklist for each individual to help maintain organization.

Tasks	Notes	Date
Write contract/agreement and deliver		
Record with agreement/ contract is signed and returned?		
Get bio, testimonials, vita		
Is the payment agreement complete?		
Are the audio visual requirements discussed and finalized?		
Are the hotel accommodations complete?		
Itinerary and agenda sent to speaker		
Transportation and travel information sent		
Copies of handouts received?		
Discuss and negotiate selling products at the event		
Have you sent the speaker packet?		
Is the evaluation form complete?		

Food and Beverage Functions

Create a checklist for each separate meal and beverage function even if it is a coffee break in the morning and one in the afternoon. Make two checklists because they will be different.

Tasks	Notes
Know what your participants want and need	
Assignment of room	
Look over menus and get bids	
Establish your food and beverage budget	
Will the price of the meal be included in the registration or separate charge?	
Create timelines for menu planning	
Meet with the chef and/or catering department	
Provide catering department with your agenda and timelines	
Decide styles of service o Buffet o Reception o Sit-down o Formal/informal o Free/limited pour for receptions	
For cocktail reception o Buffet or served o Bar setup and how many bartenders? o Charge/not charge and how for liquor	
Determine theme/decorations	

Tasks	Notes
Other considerations for food functions: o Know the liquor laws o Checkrooms o Microphones or audio visuals o Staging o Table cars o Printed menus o Gifts o Head table o Reserved tables	
Breaks needed for a.m. and p.m. – How many	
What to serve at breaks? Food and beverage?	
Vendors needed?	
How to ask guests what special dietary needs they may have?	
What kind of seating arrangement?	
Are there any renovations going on during our dates?	
Arrange with the food and beverage department a pre-event meeting.	
Decide number of staff or volunteers needed.	
How much ice needed if outside?	
Take into consideration our environmental standards when choosing menu and drinks	
What to do with leftover food?	
Have we looked at cost cutting suggestions?	

Quick Reference Guide Food and Beverage Servings

Keep these handy formulas for quickly creating the food and beverage needs of your participants. Coffee Breaks and Continental Breakfasts.

Morning	Afternoon	Coffee
• 65% hot	• 35% hot	• 18-20 cups per gallon
• 35% cold beverages	• 65% cold beverages	• 14-16 cups per gallon (mugs)
• 50-75% diet soft drinks	• 50-75% diet soft drinks	• 60% regular
• 25% regular soft drinks	• 25% regular soft drinks	• 40% decaf

Alcohol Service

These are standard amounts and will change depending on your specific group.

- Three bottles per table of eight (two white & one red) with dinner

- Five 5 oz. glasses per 750 ml bottle

- Ten 5 oz. glasses per 1.5 liter magnum

- Count one half bottle per person with a 10 percent cushion

- Consumption of white wine is higher in the summer and more red wine in the winter

- For every ten bottles of white or sparkling wine have two bottles of red (opposite if red meat entree)

- Your wine cost should not exceed 20 percent of the total food and beverage cost

- You will get 21-25 drinks per bottle of liquor

- If you are serving both hard liquor and beer and wine it will be about half will want hard and half soft

- Women consume more wine than liquor

- Cash Bar after a meeting — 50 percent will stay and have 1.5 drinks (1 hour reception)

- Hosted Bar — Cocktail Hour: 80 percent will stay and have 2 to 2-½ drinks in 1 hour and 3 to 3-½ drinks in 1-½ hours

Receptions

- 6-8 hors d'oeuvres pieces per person per hour if reception is prior to dinner

- 10-12 hors d'oeuvres pieces per person per hour if reception is in place of dinner

- Typical wine consumption is three glasses during a two-hour reception

Room Set Up and Audio Visual Needs

Create a checklist for each separate room where audio visual needs are required.

Tasks	Notes
Talk with speakers/entertainers about their needs	
Talk with and/or meet with audio/visual and Technical department	
Received bids from outside vendors	
Put costs in budget	
Review and sign contract	
Decide what you need and how many. • Internet Access • LCD Projector • Slide projector • Overhead projects • How many microphones • Panel table needed • Staging • Movie Projector • Wide Screens • Spotlights • Special Effects • Easel Pad and markers • Audio or video taped sessions • Webcasting or podcasting ability • Simulcasts needed for additional rooms	
What are your lighting needs?	
Do you need walkie talkies?	
Speak with the Banquet team for room setup • Rounds • Banquet • Theatre • Conference • Classroom • Reception • U-shaped • Staging	

Complete Room Set-up

The following table can be used when all food and beverages, room setup and audio visual equipment requirements are known. This is a good reference table to use for you, your volunteers, the venue, and staff.

Thursday, January 26, 2007					
Room Name	**Time**	**Event**	**Setup**	**Audio/Visual**	**Food and Beverage**
Marin A Check room at 10:30 a.m.	11 a.m. – 2 p.m.	Lunch—Keynote speaker Ms. Morgan	Rounds for 100 13 tables with linens 8 chairs per table	2 lavaliere mics Stage Podium 2 rectangle tables with skirt Internet access LCD Projector Handouts	Lunch for 100 Chicken with veggies Ice Tea and Lemonade
Sonoma B	8 a.m. – 5:30 p.m.	Meeting Ms. Saks	Theatre Style	Internet access LCD Projector Podium Easel and Pad with markers	N/A
Foyer in front of Sonoma B and Napa C	8 a.m. – 11:30 Break at 10:30 – 11:00 a.m.	Coffee break at 10:30	4 8' rectangles with skirts	N/A	2 gallon coffee 1 gal decaf 1 gal hot water with tea bags 5 dozen Danish

Thursday, January 26, 2007					
Room Name	**Time**	**Event**	**Setup**	**Audio/Visual**	**Food and Beverage**
Napa C	8 a.m. – 5:30 p.m.	Meeting Ms. Currey	Classroom Style	Internet access LCD Projector Podium Easel and Pad with markers Overhead Projector	N/A
Marin A	5 p.m. – 10 p.m.	Dinner and panel Mr. Guy Ms. Alexander Mr. McGreen Ms. Kimball	Rounds 13 tables with linens – blue napkins and flower bouquet 8 chairs per table	2 lavaliere mics 2 table top mics Stage Podium 4 rectangle tables with skirts	Dinner for 100 Steak with asparagus Ice Tea 2 bottles red wine per table 1 bottle white wine per table Orange sherbet for dessert.

Registration Set-Up

Tasks	Notes
Develop registration system or select suitable registration software for data base	
Enter data: Conference name, dates, location, tracks, social events, exhibitors, speakers	
Enter registrants: name, company, address, telephone, fax, e-mail, fee payment method	
Decide payment process for deposit, credit cards, checks, etc.	
Forward confirmation, acknowledgements, and/or appropriate communications regarding receipt of registration	
For those who owe money, prepare special correspondence on a regular basis until paid or in accordance with the stated agreement	
For cancellations, refunds, and other customer services, retrieve records, enter requested charges, acknowledge, and process refund if required	
Print badges	
Prepare on-site registration lists	
Prepare and/or include in on-site packages the certifications of attendance	
Prepare/train on-site registration staff, adhering to policies	
Review on-site logistics, signs, and traffic flow	
Prepare a help desk	
Prepare supply of registrations forms for on-site registration for walk-ins	
Process on-site registrations	
Process all money collected on-site	
Check collections and do cleanup: letters to no-shows and to those who still owe money	
Do the final accounting, reconciliation, and reports	

Designing Your Promotional Material

Remember to create material with attention, interest, desire to promote action through the use of strong and inviting verbiage.

Tasks	Notes
Prepare a budget for promotional materials	
Decide the methods of promotion and create material for each style	
Create timelines for materials	
Find printer and or Web designer—get bids	
Look into professional mailing companies	
Begin designing material	
Decide on artwork and colors	
Design logo if needed	
Name event	
Prepare production schedule	
Create registration form or sign up sheets both for Web and paper	
Proof and then proof again all the material	
Decide method of promotion • Mailing Lists • E-mail Lists • Brochure • Advertising • Flyers • Telephone solicitation • Save the date cards • Web based	
Send material to printer either by hard copy or electronically	
Sort, distribute, deliver, mail, pass out, e-mail, promotions.	
Have system for immediate RSVP's or registration or ticket sales.	

Fact Sheet Following the Event

Statistics	Notes
Name of Event:	
Event Coordinator(s):	
Defined Vision:	
Goals and Objectives:	
Dates:	
Destination:	
Venues:	
Number of participants:	
Sleeping rooms used:	
Transportation used:	
Theme:	
Food and beverage used:	
Marketing efforts:	
Fees for participants:	
Budget:	
Speakers:	
Topics:	
Agenda:	
Meeting rooms:	
Exhibits:	
Special Events:	

Environmental Checklist for Venue Selection

This list is quite extensive, but when you created your own environmental standards you will know which of the following questions and answers pertain to you.

Item/Question	Yes	No	Notes
Does property purchase reusable, recycled and durable products, or products that can be recycled?			
Does property have an in-house recycling program for both the property and guests? What materials are collected?			
Does property recycle any other materials (linens, phone books, oil, pallets, batteries)?			
Will your property provide recycling bins for our meeting? What materials will have recycling bins: aluminum, glass, newspaper, white paper, plastic, steel cans.			
Will property commit to seeing that the above items collected from our meeting are actually recycled?			
Does property have a contract with recycling haulers or businesses?			
Does property donate, sell, or recycle old durables (i.e., furnishings, etc.)?			

Item/Question	Yes	No	Notes
Will your food and beverage services use reusable items such as cloth, glass, ceramic rather than disposable items such as styrofoam or plastic for our meeting?			
Will your property serve food buffet-style? One large plate? Without garnishes?			
Will your property use cream pitchers, sugar pourers, and washable spoons rather than individual creamer and sugar packets for our meeting? Jelly servers rather than individual packets?			
Will your kitchen purchase fresh rather than packaged produce?			
Are vegetarian or vegan menus available?			
Does your property purchase and serve beverages from a dispenser or in returnable refillable containers?			
Who pays for bottle deposits—the client or the property?			
Does your property donate leftover food to a local non-profit organization?			
Will you provide cloth rather than disposable table drapes for display tables?			
Does your property have props, decorations, foliage or centerpieces that we can use?			

Item/Question	Yes	No	Notes
Will your property use chips or coins rather than disposable paper tickets for coat checking and auto parking?			
Does your property have guestroom dispensers for soap and shampoo?			
Is property willing to remove all small plastic amenity bottles from the guestrooms which our participants will occupy?			
Does property give guests a choice on having bath linens and bed sheets exchanged?			
Do guestrooms have low-flow showerheads? Low-flow sink aerators?			
Will pitchers of water be placed on the tables rather than glasses of water?			
Will you use insulated water containers to keep the water cold longer?			
Will you use water from a cooler rather than using ice?			
Will you use leftover water and ice to water plants and replenish fountains?			
What other water conservation measures have been taken?			
What are you doing to reduce dry cleaning and laundry paraphernalia?			
Does property offer double-sided copying at a reduced rate?			

Item/Question	Yes	No	Notes
Do doors to your meeting rooms open and close silently?			
At the close of our meeting, is your property willing to distribute meeting materials and sample products left behind to a local charity that can put them to good use?			
What percentage of your property's lighting is fluorescent?			
Do meeting rooms have dimmers on lights?			
Do meeting rooms have windows for natural lighting?			
What other energy conservation measures have been taken?			
What other conservation measures have you incorporated?			
Is there anything further in regard to being "green" that your property will offer us?			

Sample Speaker Agreement

Title of Event:

Date of Speaking Engagement:

Place of Event:

Date:	Organization:
Name:	Title:
Address:	
City, State, Zip:	
Title of Session:	Start Time:
Date of Session:	End Time:

We are excited to have you speak/present/hold workshop at our next annual _____ _____. In exchange for your time and expertise you will receive the following: (put in what you will offer)

Roundtrip airfare

Hotel Room for two nights—the night prior to and night of your speaking engagement

All meals for two days (or dinner, breakfast, lunch, dinner, breakfast, lunch)

Registration for entire conference

Per Diem in the amount of $_____

Speaking fee of $_____

We will be happy to copy your handout materials (set limit) if you provided an original to us at least two weeks prior to your presentation. We will also provide you with audio-visual equipment you may need for your presentation. (You might limit if your budget is tight). You may add your environmental standard here if you have one regarding handout usage such as two-sided printing on recycled paper or keeping number of pages down.

Please send us your bio/vita to include in our promotion material as soon as possible.

Let us know soon your audio visual requirements. Check the following items needed. Please be specific and only choose what you will really need. If you will be using a computerized presentation, please bring your own laptop.

- ❑ Flipchart
- ❑ Internet Connection
- ❑ LCD projector
- ❑ VCR/DVD and monitor
- ❑ Overhead projector and screen
- ❑ Other _____
- ❑ Slide projector
- ❑ Wireless Microphone

You are responsible for making your airline reservations and taxi/shuttle arrangements. We will make the hotel reservations for you. Enclosed is a working draft of the agenda for the conference.

I hereby agree to present at the <name of meeting>. I affirm that, to my knowledge, none of the material presented, either verbally or in written materials, infringes upon any copyright or any person's right of privacy. I will not libel or slander any other person, facility, company, product, or service during my presentation. If such affirmation is breached, I indemnify and hold harmless <insert company> and all contracted service providers.

I also understand I cannot make a "sales pitch" or I can make a sales pitch and sell books for any specific firm, publication, or service during my presentation. I can provide participants with an opportunity to purchase publications or materials at the conclusion of my session.

_____I agree to have my session audio taped and the tapes reproduced for sale with the proceeds going to <insert who>.

Accepted:

Date:

Print Name:

Please fax or mail this agreement with your bio/vita to: <phone, address>

$\mathscr{T}imelines$

Timeline for Smaller Events

Make sure all the tasks connected with your type of event are included. Make it as comprehensive as possible.

TIME FRAME	TO DO LIST / TASKS	DONE	NOTES
3 months out (Put in actual dates)	Hold committee/staff meeting – define goals and objectives, financial goals – defined vision		
	Review roles and responsibilities		
	Create budget, define audience		
Ten weeks out	Secure site/facility, sign contracts		
	Start promotional material		
Nine weeks	Secure speaker or entertainment		
Eight weeks	Start preparing menus		
	Design layout		
Seven weeks	Determine meeting format		
	Complete contract agreements		
	Edit promotional material		
Six weeks	Approve promotional material		
	Secure travel arrangements/ information		
	Order food and beverage and A/V needs		
Five weeks	Print material and send out/place ad/put up flyers		
	Make travel arrangements for speakers/staff		
	Secure sleeping rooms		

TIME FRAME	TO DO LIST / TASKS	DONE	NOTES
Four weeks	Buy name badges/gifts/ memorabilia		
	Confirm number of participants to appropriate people		
	Order flower / decorations		
Three weeks	Pay all deposits required		
Two weeks	Confirm participants		
	Finalize order for F/B and A/V		
	Finalize any travel arrangements		
	Create name badges / lists and signs		
One week out	Ship materials to site		
	Send final numbers of participants for /F/B, A/V		
	Rehearse on-site personnel		
	Review all confirmations		
Day before	Review all events, do a run through		
	Establish on-site presence		
	Hold pre-conference with faculty		
	Check to see if all your materials have arrived		
	Set up registration		

Large Event Timeline

Coordination of very large events will sometimes begin two to three years in advance especially when booking a venue and entertainment. Just change the dates accordingly and create a timeline that is unique to your event.

TIME FRAME	TO DO LIST / TASKS	DONE	NOTES
1 year out (Put in your actual dates)	Hold committee/staff meeting, define goals and objectives, create roles and responsibilities		
	Choose Destination – City, State		
	Meet with event planner and others to review roles and responsibilities		
	Confirm financial goals and objectives		
	Prepare budget		
	Choose location – venue		
	Confirm dates and times		
11 months	Conduct site inspection		
10 months	Secure facility / sign contracts		
9 months	Begin researching for speakers and entertainment		
	List subjects for agenda		
8 months	Draft topics and agenda		
7 months	Confirm speakers/entertainment		
6 months	Begin design of promotional material		
	Get quotes for printed material		
5 months	Develop guest list		
	Confirm hotel		
	Edit materials		
	Start F/B and A/V process		
4 months	Pay all deposits required		
	Final design to printer		

TIME FRAME	TO DO LIST / TASKS	DONE	NOTES
3 months	Material to mail house		
	Meeting with meeting planner and others to review roles and responsibilities		
	Review budget		
	Determine meeting format		
	Complete contract agreements		
	Develop promotional material		
	Secure travel arrangements/ information		
	Approve promotional material		
	Hire photographer, other services and vendors		
Five weeks	Complete meeting materials		
	Confirm volunteers and the responsibilities		
Four weeks	Order signs		
	Make sure all contracts are signed		
	Print meeting materials		
	Confirm travel arrangements for speakers/staff		
Three weeks	Complete any additional printed material		
	Review everything		
	Confirm number participants		
	Finalize F/B menus		
	Get a massage		
Two weeks out	Buy last office supplies for event		
	Finalize everything		
	Ship materials to site		
	Send final numbers for participants/ F/B, A/V		

TIME FRAME	TO DO LIST / TASKS	DONE	NOTES
One week	Prepare welcome letters, certificates		
	Print name badges		
	Rehearse on-site personnel		
	Prepare tool kit		
Night/Day before	Arrive on-site, establish on-site presence		
	Hold pre-conference with faculty		
	Set up registration area		
	Prepare binder		
Day of Event	Have tool kit		
	Have binder		
	Station volunteers		
	Check all equipment and F/B lists		
After Event	Thank you notes – gifts – tips and gratuities		
	Create final report/summary		
	Review and summarize evaluations		
	Review and finalize budget		
	Pay last of the bills due		

Author
Biography

*A*t an early age Shannon Kilkenny began what would become her career in event planning by gathering her neighborhood friends on a regular basis. Throughout high school and college she volunteered for committees and headed organizations allowing her to bring people together for a variety of reasons. Concurrently, she began a writing career with newsletters, articles, copy for marketing material, and later writing and editing guidebooks, user manuals, and how-to books. These two careers continue in concert for more than 25 years.

Her expertise and good humor created successful business relationships with clients in the banking industry, hospitality trade, educational and non-profit organizations, professional associations, athletic clubs and the environmental community. Having participated with these diverse  groups, Ms. Kilkenny is familiar with multiple segments of the business and social world.

With the writing and event planning skills strongly embedded and using her multi-layered experiences, the book, *The Complete Guide to Successful Event Planning*, was born.

She is currently teaching event planning classes, workshops and seminars, and doing public speaking. She developed a curriculum for all levels of commitment. She has mentored beginners through their first event and assisted seasoned professionals seeking new heights of proficiency.

Her latest endeavor for event planning is to help the industry create new environmental standards. She is in the process of writing her next book dedicated to "greening" the hospitality and event planning business.

In her leisure time you will find her in her garden, in her kayak, or in the clutches of a good book. Ms. Kilkenny lives by the ocean North of San Francisco. 🐋

Glossary

– A –

à la carte - Each item is priced and sold individually on the menu.

Act of God Clause or Force Majeure - A part of a contract that releases both parties from liability due to circumstances beyond their control. Examples are tornadoes, war, and famine.

Adult Learning Techniques - Methods used to teach and re-train individuals who are returning to an educational setting.

Agenda - An outline of the meeting schedule or the detailed task list for an event.

Amenity - An item placed in a guestroom such as food, beverages, or some other gift. In-room amenities are also shampoos and bathrobes.

American Plan - A hotel rate plan that covers sleeping room and all meals.

Americans with Disabilities Act of 1990 (ADA) - A federal law that outlines clear and comprehensive prohibition of discrimination on the basis of disability. Both planners and suppliers must provide reasonable accommodations to such persons. **www.usdoj.gov/crt/ada/adahom1.htm**

American Society of Association Executives (ASAE) - Association for managers and executives of associations. **www.asae.org**

American Society of Composers, Authors and Publishers (ASCAP) - Association that licenses and distributes royalties for the non-dramatic public performances of copyrighted works. **www.ascap.com**

Appliqué - A small, self-stick, embroidered design used for name badges, lapels, and clothes. Used for themes and identifiers.

Arbitration - A procedure devised to resolve a contractual dispute outside of the court system.

Arrival Pattern - Specific days and time blocks when attendees are expected to arrive.

Association - An organization made up of people with common goals or who are in the same industry.

Association Planner - Individuals who plan meetings for associations.

Attendee - A participant in your event.

Attrition - A reduction in numbers from the figure you promised the meeting facility.

The numbers are the guestrooms, food, beverage, and meal covers from which the facility forecasts its potential revenue and profit. Attrition is also called slippage or drop-off.

Audio-Visual (A-V) - Equipment and resources devoted to helping attendees hear and see the meeting.

Authorized Signature - Signature from the person designated with legal authority to enter into a binding agreement.

– ℬ –

Backdrop - Background of a stage set.

Back of the House - The area in a meeting facility that the staff uses. It is not open to the public.

Bandwidth - The data transmission capacity of an electronic line. It is expressed in bits per second (BPS).

Banquet - A fancy meal. It is usually used for special occasions.

Banquet Check - The standard document used to break down the charges for a specific event, usually food and beverage charges.

Banquet Event Order (BEO) or Banquet Prospectus - Hotel information sheet for staff listing the details of a meal function including times, number of people, menu, special instructions, audio-visual equipment, and billing information.

Bid - A written or verbal statement that describes what you will do in response to an offer (or a request for bid).

Book - To make an advanced reservation.

Booking Pattern - Arrival and departure days of the week for a group or individuals.

Booth - An area made up of tables or stands that is used to sell or display materials. The area is usually decorated or partitioned to draw attention to it.

BPS rate- Bits per second is a measure of the number of data bits (digital 0s and 1s) transmitted each second in a communications channel, usually refers to modem speed.

Break-even Point - The point at which your meeting neither makes nor loses money.

Breakout Session - A spin-off group from a large meeting with presentations focused on a specific topic.

Budget - Financial sheets that provide line items for each potential meeting expense.

Business Casual - A casual style of dress for business functions. Jeans, tennis shoes, sandals, and shorts are not included.

Butlered Service - Servers carry trays of food and drinks to offer to guests. Used mostly for receptions.

Buyers Market - A business climate in which supply exceeds demand.

– *C* –

Cafeteria Service - Food service by attendants from a buffet table or line.

Call Brand - A medium priced brand of alcohol.

Call for Presentation - An application for the opportunity to be a presenter at a meeting or conference. Conference organizers are usually looking for specific topics, and carefully following the application guidelines gives the applicant a better chance of being selected.

Cancellation Clause - Terms in a contract that describe what each party will provide/receive if the contract is terminated.

Cash Bar - Bar service where attendees pay for their own drinks.

Catering Manager - Person who plans and manages meal functions at a hotel.

Certified Meeting Professional (CMP) - A professional certification for meeting professionals, both planners and suppliers.

Classroom Style or Schoolroom - A room set with rows of tables and chairs facing the presenter.

City-wide - Large meetings that cannot be held in only one location. Attendees stay in hotels throughout the city and usually meet at a large convention center or venue.

Coach - An individual with experience and leadership who guides people and helps them achieve specific goals. Also, another name for motor coach.

Colloquium - An academic presentation about a specialized topic usually to a group of colleagues.

Commissionable Rate - A guestroom rate in which the hotel agrees to pay a specific percentage back to a designated organization. An industry standard for third-party meeting planners and travel agents is 10 percent. A net rate is void of any commissions.

Comp - Short for complimentary or free.

Company Meeting - A meeting for people from the same company or organization. These include board, staff, and sales meetings and focus on information exchange, problem solving, and decision making.

Concierge - A hotel staff person who handles special requests by guests such as dinner reservations, social events, directions, and laundry.)

Concession - Yielding on a point to reach agreement.

Concurrent Session - Simultaneous meetings.

Conference - Meetings for people who have a shared discipline or industry, usually for educational reasons.

Conference Center - A facility designed specifically to house meetings with limited or no sleeping rooms.

Conference Style - A seating arrangement with chairs placed around all sides of a table.

Confirmation - Verification of a reservation. Also a verification of any commitment to a facility, attendee, or speaker.

Congress - The act of coming together in a meeting; a formal meeting of delegates.

Continental Breakfast - Abbreviated breakfast that consists of coffee, tea, juice, pastries and breads.

Contingency Plans - Written documents prepared in advance addressing every conceivable emergency or other urgent issue.

Continuing Education Units (CEUs) - A requirement of many professional associations that individuals earn a specific number of CEUs to maintain their original certification status.

Contract - A binding agreement between two or more persons or parties that is legally enforceable.

Convention - Describes an assembly of delegates who formulate a platform and select candidates and/or take legal action. They also focus on a common topic or issue.

Convention and Visitors Bureau (CVB) - Not-for-profit organizations representing destinations. They are typically funded by a combination of membership dues, taxes, and government funding. Their members are organizations who provide products and services to planners such as hotels, restaurants and attractions.

Convention Industry Council (CIC) - Consists of numerous organizations representing the convention, meeting, and exhibition industry as well as travel and tourism generally. **www.conventionindustry.org**

Convention Services Manager (CSM) - Person who plans and manages meeting details at a hotel.

Corporate Planner - Individual who plans meetings for corporations.

Cover - A meal served to one attendee. If you serve 200 people for dinner, you serve 200 covers.

Crudités - An hor d'oeuvre display of raw vegetables usually served with a dip.

Cut-Off Date – The date the hotel releases your room block back to general inventory.

– *𝒟* –

Dais - A raised platform in a large room, usually where speakers and honored guests are seated.

Damage Clause - Terms in a contract that describe the procedures, fees, and rights of the party causing damages.

Data Record - The unique collection of information about a specific object.

Destination Management Company (DMC) - Companies available to help planners in a destination or city. They can arrange tours, plan and manage your meeting, plan a themed event, conduct a spouse or guest program, among other things

Digital Subscriber Line (DSL) – A line that allows a modem to transform a plain telephone service line into a digital line and thus beef up bandwidth capability.

Double Booking - When two or more groups or individuals are promised the same space for the same time.

Drayage - The service that includes delivery of materials to an exhibit space, removal of empty crates, storage of crates during the function, returning of crates at the end of the function, and delivery of materials to the carrier loading area.

Dual Projection – The projection of two images simultaneously using two projectors and two screens.

– *ℰ* –

Easel - A tripod stand for displaying signs or flipcharts.

English Breakfast - A full breakfast that includes stations for made-to-order food.

Entrée - The main course of a meal.

Evaluation - Written feedback of a meeting or event from attendees, sponsors, exhibitors and organizers.

Event Order or Function Sheet - A document outlining all of the details of a specific event. Includes, location, times, head counts, audio-visuals, and food and beverage.

Exhibitor - Person or group who displays products or services at a trade show or exhibition.

Exhibit Manager - A person in charge of the company's exhibit program.

Exhibitor Service Kit or Service Kit - A package of information that contains the rules, regulations, and forms relating to an exhibition. It is provided to exhibitors by company supplying the services for the trade show.

Exposition of Exhibition - Booth-type format to display services and products to consumers and public.

Exposition Services Contractor or Decorator - The company that provides the booth, signs, setup, and other services needed for a trade show or exposition.

Facilitator - A person designated to make a meeting run effectively and smoothly.

Facility - A building or venue designed for a specific purpose.

Familiarization Trip (FAM Trip) - A trip hosted by a destination or a CVB and its members for the sole purpose of showcasing the city or venue as an event location.

Fiber Optic Circuit - Data connectivity services for higher-bandwidth applications. It is a hair-thin glass strand designed for light transmission. It is capable of transmitting trillions of bits per second.

Fixed Expenses - Expenses that will remain constant no matter how many participants attend.

Flip Chart - An oversized notepad of paper on an easel used to make notes during a meeting for attendees to see.

First Option - Term used to describe a group's reservation for space at a property. Used when the space is being held and waiting for a contract to be signed. If another group wants to hold the same space, they would have second option.

Food and Beverage Minimum - An amount you are required to spend for food and beverages, not including taxes, gratuities, or service charges. If you spend below the amount, you pay the difference between the minimum and the actual amount spent.

Force Majeure - A legal concept in contractual law. Force Majeure negates the need to perform under a contract when events beyond the control of either party make it impossible to do so. Examples are tornadoes and war. Also called Act of God Clause.

French Service - A type of food service in which a server places the food on a plate from a prepared platter.

Function - A specific component of a meeting such as a meal, breakout session, registration, or off-site tour.

Function Books - Schedule books for reserving meeting space in a hotel.

Function Sheet or Event Order - A document that outlines all of the details of a specific event. Includes, location, times, head counts, audio-visuals, food, and beverage.

Function Space - The physical space where the function takes place.

– G –

General Session - Meeting format that addresses all attendees.

Goal - The foundation of a meeting. It explains why the meeting is being held and provides a road map for the planning process.

Gratuity - A voluntary amount of money given in exchange for a service performed. Also referred to as a "tip."

Group History or History - Specific information about a group's prior meetings. History covers room pickup, revenue, dates, pattern, problems, and other important details.

Guarantee - The number of people you tell the property is attending a meal function— usually required 36-72 hours prior to the function.

– H –

Hold All Space - All meeting space in the hotel is being held by a group. If you have a "hold all space," it should be stated in the contract with a deadline for submitting your agenda.

Half-round - A seating arrangement with chairs placed around half of a round table so they face the presentation area.

Head count - The actual number of people at the event.

Head Table - Table reserved for VIPs, speakers, and dignitaries.

Hollow Circle - A seating arrangement with chairs facing each other in a single circle.

Hors d'oeuvres - Both hot and cold finger food served at receptions.

Horseshoe Seating - A seating arrangement with tables and chairs placed in an oblong semi-circle with one end open toward the presentation area.

Hospitality Suite - A room or suite especially in a hotel set aside as a place for socializing especially for business purposes. Food and beverages are often available.

Hosted Bar or Open Bar - Bar service paid for by a host or sponsor.

Housing Bureau - A company or organization that handles only the housing arrangements for a meeting. Usually employed for large meetings with several hotels to choose from.

Housing List - The list of attendees staying at a property. It is provided by the property and usually outlines check-in, check-out, payment info, and room type.

HSIA - High Speed Internet Access.

I-Mag or Image Magnification - A projection that allows an image to appear on a large screen allowing large groups to see the detail.

Incidentals - Additional costs that can be charged to your hotel bill such as in-room movies, mini-bar, telephone, and room service.

In Conjunction With (ICW) - An event or function that occurs because of another meeting, but may not be a part of the original meeting.

Indemnify - To secure against hurt, loss, or damage.

Indemnification - An agreement in which one party agrees to protect the other party from liability, damages, or out-of-pocket expenses that may occur in connection with a particular transaction.

Independent Planner - Individual who plans meetings for various organizations on a contract basis.

In-kind Donations - Donation of a product or service that would normally be purchased.

Internet Service Provider (ISP) – Provides connection to the Internet.

Inquiry Call - Initial contact with a supplier or vendor with the purpose of asking about their product or service.

Inventory List - A detailed list of items available, usually equipment.

– 𝒦 –

Keynote Speaker - Presenter who talks about the primary issues.

Kiosks - An interactive kiosk is an electronic communications tool that enables customers to serve themselves by accessing information, taking advantage of special offers, making purchases, or gathering information.

– 𝓛 –

Lanyard - A necklace or neck cord that attaches to the name badge so it can be hung around a person's neck.

Lavaliere Microphone - A small microphone that can be attached to clothing, allowing hands to be free.

Lead - An inquiry about placing a meeting at a specific location.

Learner Outcomes - Synonymous with "course objectives."

Lectern - A stand used to support papers and notes in a convenient position for a standing reader or presenter.

Liability Clause - Part of a contract that outlines the conditions of liability.

Liquidated Damage(s) - The amount of money that is owed by the party deemed to have breached one or some of the contractual terms. Liquidated damages are not penalties, but are compensation for lost revenue or expenses.

– 𝓜 –

Marshaling Yard - An area away from the facility where exhibitors wait to be called to the dock for loading or unloading.

Master Bill - The detailed accounting of all charges for a meeting provided by the facility.

Meet-and-Greet - Commonly used at airports to meet special passengers and either direct them to ground transportation or take them to their final destination.

Meeting - Congregation of two or more people together to further a common cause.

Meeting History - Statistical record of a past meeting or event to include guest rooms used, food, beverage, functions, and other meeting data.

Meeting Management Company - Company that provide full service meeting management services to organizations.

Meeting Manager - Person who organizes, plans, and executes activities for individuals who meet for a common cause.

Meeting or Convention Resume – Information sheet for hotel staff regarding the entire meeting which outlines the VIPs, agenda, contact information, rooming list, group profile.

Meeting Professional - Individual who plans and provides services for meetings and events.

Meeting Professionals International (MPI) - Largest association for meeting professionals. **www.mpiweb.org**

Meetings Industry - The collective resources that design, implement, and support meetings and events.

Milestone - A significant point in a process or development. Missing a milestone usually has significant consequences.

MIMlist - An online discussion group moderated by a well-known leading educator and expert in the meetings industry.

Modified American Plan - A hotel rate plan where the daily rate covers breakfast and dinner, but not lunch.

Monitor - Someone who introduces the speaker, keeps the meeting on track, gets help with audio-visual equipment if needed, and distributes and collects the evaluations (if applicable). The monitor is often a volunteer.

Move-in - Time frame in which exhibitors set up their exhibits.

Move-out - Time frame in which exhibitors break down their exhibits.

Multimedia - Using, involving, or encompassing several media such as sight and sound.

Mutual Indemnification - A term that means both parties will be responsible for their own negligent acts or omissions if they cause a loss to the other party or cause the other party to defend itself against an asserted claim in connection with a particular transaction.

National Sales Office (NSO) - A sales office for hotel companies that represents all of their properties and facilities.

Net Square Foot - The method by which some facilities charge for exhibit space. Net square footage is the space the exhibitors actually use — not including aisles, pillars, food stations, and seating.

No-Show - A person who has a reservation for a hotel room and does not show up.

– O –

Objective - A measurable, attainable target which when completed, contributes to the accomplishment of the goal.

Off-season - The time of year when the average business activity is slow.

Omnidirectional Microphone - A microphone designed to pickup sound from all directions.

On Consumption - To charge only for the items consumed. This mostly applies to food and beverage items.

On-site - Describes location of a person, function, or thing.

One-stop Shop - Obtaining meeting and meal functions from only one supplier.

Open Bar or Hosted Bar - Bar service paid for by a sponsor or host.

Outcome Objective - Relates to the needs of a meeting's attendees.

Outside Vendor - Suppliers who are not directly associated with the hotel or facility.

Outsource - To solicit and hire services from outside a company, group, or organization.

Overbooking - A practice of hotel to oversell its sleeping rooms in anticipation of no-shows.

Overflow - To fill a space beyond capacity.

– P –

Panel Discussion - Several experts deliver brief presentations in a question and answer format.

Peak Room Night - Number of hotel room nights used on the busiest night of the meeting.

Peak Season - The time of year when the average business activity is at its highest.

Pickup - Number of sleeping rooms actually used during a meeting, both daily and cumulatively.

Pickup Report - A post meeting report that outlines the number of sleeping rooms used each day of a meeting.

Pipe and Drape - Tubing covered with draped fabric to make up the rails and back wall of a trade show.

Plated Buffet - Food is pre-plated and taken by guests from the buffet table.

Plenary Sessions - Another name for a general session for all participants, usually used for medical and scientific meetings.

Podcasting - The distribution of audio or video files, such as radio programs, lectures and classes, or music videos over the Internet for listening on mobile devices (such as iPods) and personal computers.

Podium - A small raised platform for a presenter to stand on.

Portable Media Player - A PMP is a handheld audio-video system that can record and playback from TV, DVD player, camera, or media file downloaded from Internet such as iPods, MP3 players, and other mobile devices.

Post-Convention Meeting or Post Con - A meeting with the host facility's staff just after the conclusion of the conference or meeting to review the meeting.

Poster Session - A display method where posters or displays are placed on poster boards. The presenter stands in front of the poster to describe the material and answer questions.

Pre-convention Meeting or Pre Con - A meeting with the host facility's staff just before the conference.

Pre-prints - A bound copy of all the handouts and papers for every session usually provided at medical and scientific conferences where the sessions are technical.

Premium Brand - The most expensive, highest quality brand of alcohol.

Preset - Items, usually food, that are placed on tables before guests arrive. Best for salads and desserts.

Process Objective - Describes the "how-to" approach for accomplishing something.

Proposal - An offer or bid for services.

– *R* –

Rack Rate - A hotel's standard, published room rate.

RFID - Radio Frequency

Identification Device uses access points to retrieve information remotely from special tags via radio waves. It captures data from up to 15 feet away. Used on name tags for tracking.

Rear Projection - Visual image is projected from behind the screen.

Reception - A social gathering often for the purpose of extending a formal welcome.

Registrant - The person officially registered for a meeting or event, also called an attendee or participant.

Relational Database - A structured set of data made up of records so data can be searched and accessed across different databases.

Return on Investment (ROI) - The process of evaluating a meeting in terms of value to the stakeholders involved in it.

Request for Proposal (RFP) - An outline of all pertinent meeting specifications.

Reservation List - The list of reservations under a specific group's room block.

Room Block - The total number of sleeping rooms reserved for a group.

Room Capacity - The number of people a room can safely hold.

Room Nights - The number of rooms times the number of nights used during a meeting.

Room Set - The physical layout for a meeting, such as classroom, theater, and rounds.

Rooming List - A list of people you are making room reservations for. Includes check-in and out dates, room type, special comments, and billing information.

Rounds - Circular tables. Sizes vary but are usually either 60" diameter (seats 8) or 72" diameter (seats 10).

Router - A router connects the T1 to an Internet Service Provider (ISP).

Run of the House - Sleeping rooms parceled out to guests according to availability when reservations are made or during check-in.

_— 𝒮 —_

Schoolroom Style or Classroom - A room set with rows of tables and chairs facing the presenter.

Sellers Market - A business climate where the meeting facility has such strong demand that it can charge higher rates and be selective about the business it books.

Service Charge - A mandatory charge added to a service. For example, hotels often charge a flat service charge for food, beverage, and audio-visual services.

Shoulder Season - The time of year when the average business activity is low. Usually between high seasons.

Silent Auction - Raises funds by displaying items up for bid. The participants provide their bid in writing. At the end of the specified time period, the person with the highest bid keeps the item.

Site Inspection or Site Visit - A visit to a facility to determine whether it fulfills your meeting needs. Usually meet with the sales representative and convention services manager and tour much of the facility.

Six by Six Rule - An audio-visual guideline that states on overhead or slide should contain no more than six words per line and no more than six lines of text.

Slippage - A reduction in numbers from what you promised the meeting facility. The numbers are the guestrooms and food and beverage meal covers from which the facility forecasts its potential revenue and profit. Also called attrition or drop-off.

Speakers Bureau - An organization that represents professional speakers. You can use its services for free. The speaker pays the representation fee directly to the bureau.

Special Events - High profile gatherings that cover a wide variety of areas such as sporting events, fundraisers, tributes, community programs, festivals, parades, and road shows.

Specification Sheet or Spec Sheet - List of meeting rooms and the number of people they can hold in various set-ups.

Sponsor - Organization or individual who contributes money, products, or services.

Square Set - A conference-style table arrangement of double or triple wide tables.

Stakeholder - A stakeholder is someone who has a vested interest in the success of the meeting such as the vice president of the company paying the bill or a meeting sponsor.

Suppliers - Vendors and organizations that supply products and services for meetings and events.

– 𝒯 –

T1 - A high speed Internet connection which is a dedicated copper circuit installed by the telephone company. Many hotels and other large venues are equipped with this service.

Table Microphone - A microphone placed on a table for panel discussions or at a head table.

Tabletop Display - A display that sits on a table used for exhibits and informational purposes.

Target Rate - The lowest group rate available on a given day.

Teleseminar - A teleseminar is a telephone conference call. Attendees call into the teleseminar at a set time (not toll-free). The presenter calls in and begins the presentation.

Termination Clause - Part of a contract dealing with procedures, damages, and rights for terminating an agreement.

Theater Style - A seating arrangement with chairs placed side by side facing a stage or towards the speaker.

Tip - Cash or gift given to individuals to thank them for good service. Not the same as a gratuity or service charges. They are added by the facility and automatically charged. A tip is an extra reward at the discretion of the planner.

Trade Show - Booth-type format to communicate and sell services and products to members of a specific group. Also called a show.

Transient Demand - Demand for guestrooms by individual travelers.

T-Shape Set - Table arrangement that looks like a "T" from above.

– 𝒰 –

Unidirectional Microphone - A microphone designed to pick up sound from one direction.

Universal Serial Bus (USB) - Sends data to standard devices such as computers, but its popularity has prompted it to become commonplace on video game consoles, PDAs, cell phones, and even devices such as televisions, home stereo equipment (mp3 players), and portable memory devices.

USB Flash Drives - Data storage devices integrated with a USB interface. They are typically small, lightweight, removable, and re-writable.

U-Shape Set - Table arrangement that looks like a "U" from above. Also called horseshoe.

– *V* –

Variable Expenses - Expenses that fluctuate based on the number of participants.

Venue - Location of a specific function.

Virtual Community - These communities are guaranteed to play an important role in the future of the meetings industry. Technology will evolve to work better with virtual communities.

V-Shape - Table arrangement that looks like a "V" from above. Chairs are usually only on the outside.

– *W* –

Walk - A term used for a person who has a guaranteed reservation but is moved to another hotel because the hotel is overbooked. If you are walked, the facility will compensate you by taking you to another hotel and paying for the room and a phone call home. This is also known as a dishonored reservation.

Well Brand - The lowest priced brand of alcohol.

Web Casting - The transmission of linear audio or video content over the Internet. A Web cast uses streaming media technology to take a single content source and distribute it to many simultaneous listeners and viewers.

Webinars - Similar to Web casting. Used to capture a recording to use for client support archives or for use as a salable product.

Wireless - Internet wireless is a method of communication that uses low-powered radio waves to transmit data between devices. The term refers to communication without cables or cords, chiefly using radio frequency and infrared waves.

Wireless Microphone - Operated by transmitting a signal to a receiver. Wireless lavalieres are popular.

Workshop - A usually brief intensive educational program for a relatively small group of people that focuses on techniques and skills in one field.